Language Arts
Workbook B

Siegfried Engelmann

Evan Haney

Jean Osborne

Owen Engelmann

Karen Davis

Acknowledgments

The authors are grateful to the following people for their assistance in the preparations of Reading Mastery Transformations Grade 1 Language.

Cally Dwyer
Katherine Gries
Debbi Kleppen
Patricia McFadden
Piper VanNortwick

mheducation.com/prek-12

Copyright © 2021 McGraw-Hill Education

All rights reserved. No part of this publication may be reproduced or distributed in any form or by any means, or stored in a database or retrieval system, without the prior written consent of McGraw-Hill Education, including, but not limited to, network storage or transmission, or broadcast for distance learning.

Send all inquiries to:
McGraw-Hill Education
8787 Orion Place
Columbus, OH 43240

ISBN: 978-0-07-905562-0
MHID: 0-07-905562-1

Printed in the United States of America.

3 4 5 6 7 8 9 LMN 24 23 22 21

Name _____

76

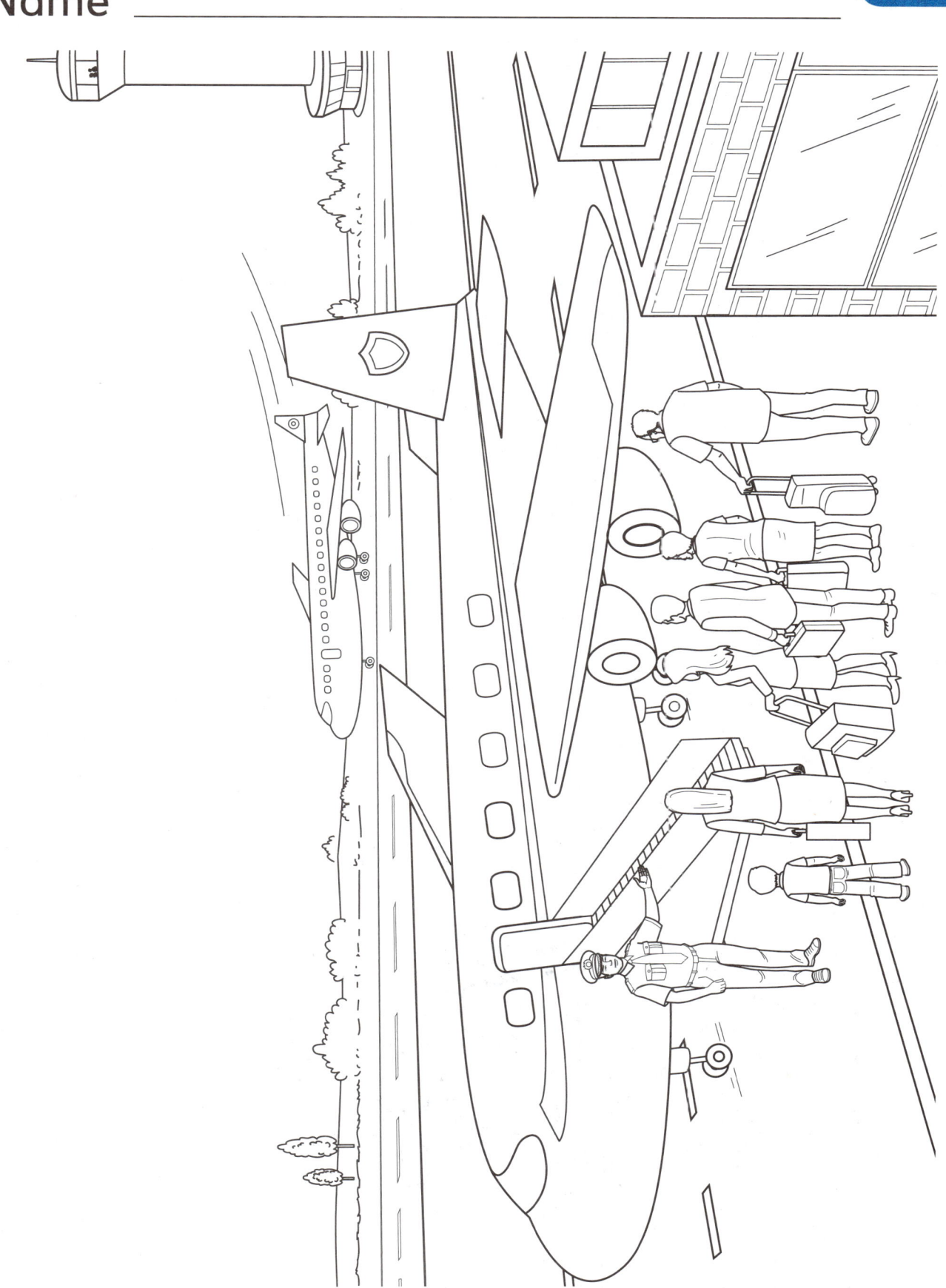

Side 1

shuttle   runway   helicopter   gravity   airport

1. Astronauts fly a _____ into space.

2. Planes land on a _____.

3. _____ keeps your feet on the ground.

4. Pilots work in an _____.

5. A _____ flies patients to a hospital.

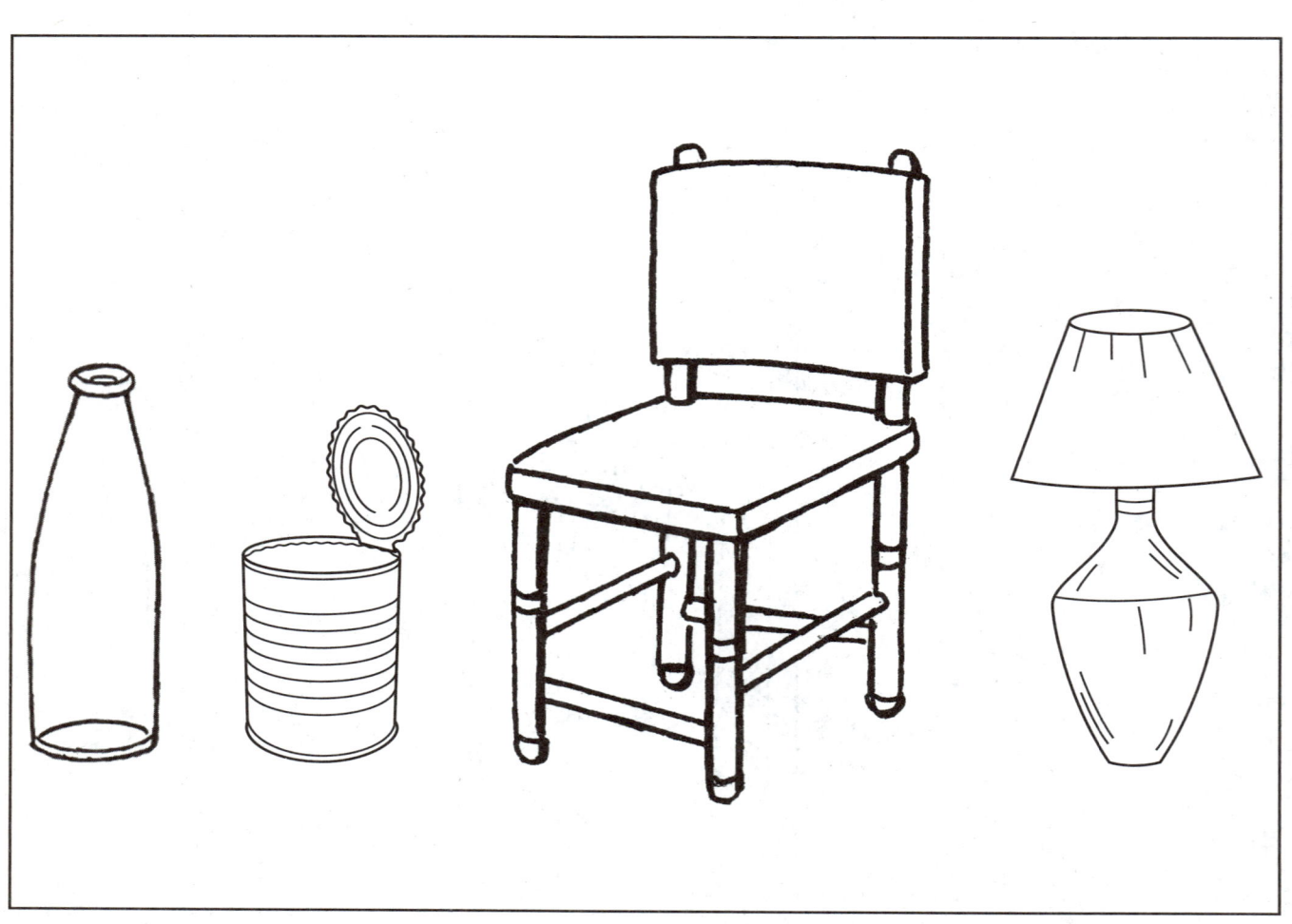

Side 2

Name _____

	True	False

1. Scissors can cut cloth. _____

2. A blanket is made of cloth. _____

3. A barn is furniture. _____

Sunday   Monday   Tuesday   Wednesday
        Thursday   Friday   Saturday

after   near   hard   deep   under   bright

1. The test was too easy for Sam's brother.

2. I found a dull penny on the floor.

3. Can we go swimming before Saturday?

Side 2

Name _____

78

Side 1

1. sara jorge and tom will come on monday

2. is frank s birthday in june or july

3. my mom thinks i am taller than dan s son

Side 2

Name _____

| vehicles   colors   plants |

truck _____   flower _____

tree _____   pink _____

ship _____   yellow _____

green _____   grass _____

plane _____   red _____

Side 1

True	False

1. Snow is hot. _____

2. You go to school to learn. _____

3. A dress is made of cloth. _____

---

fast	shallow	raw	loud	easy	difficult

1. That quick dog will win the race.
_____
_____

2. The theater was too noisy on Friday.
_____
_____

3. Do you think the test will be hard?
_____
_____

Side 2

Name _____

80

1. josh tom and i will finish in march

2. can ali s cat jump over that fence

3. we had lunch with crystal and joanne on tuesday

Side 1

January, February, March →

April, May, June →

July, August, September →

October, November, December →

Name

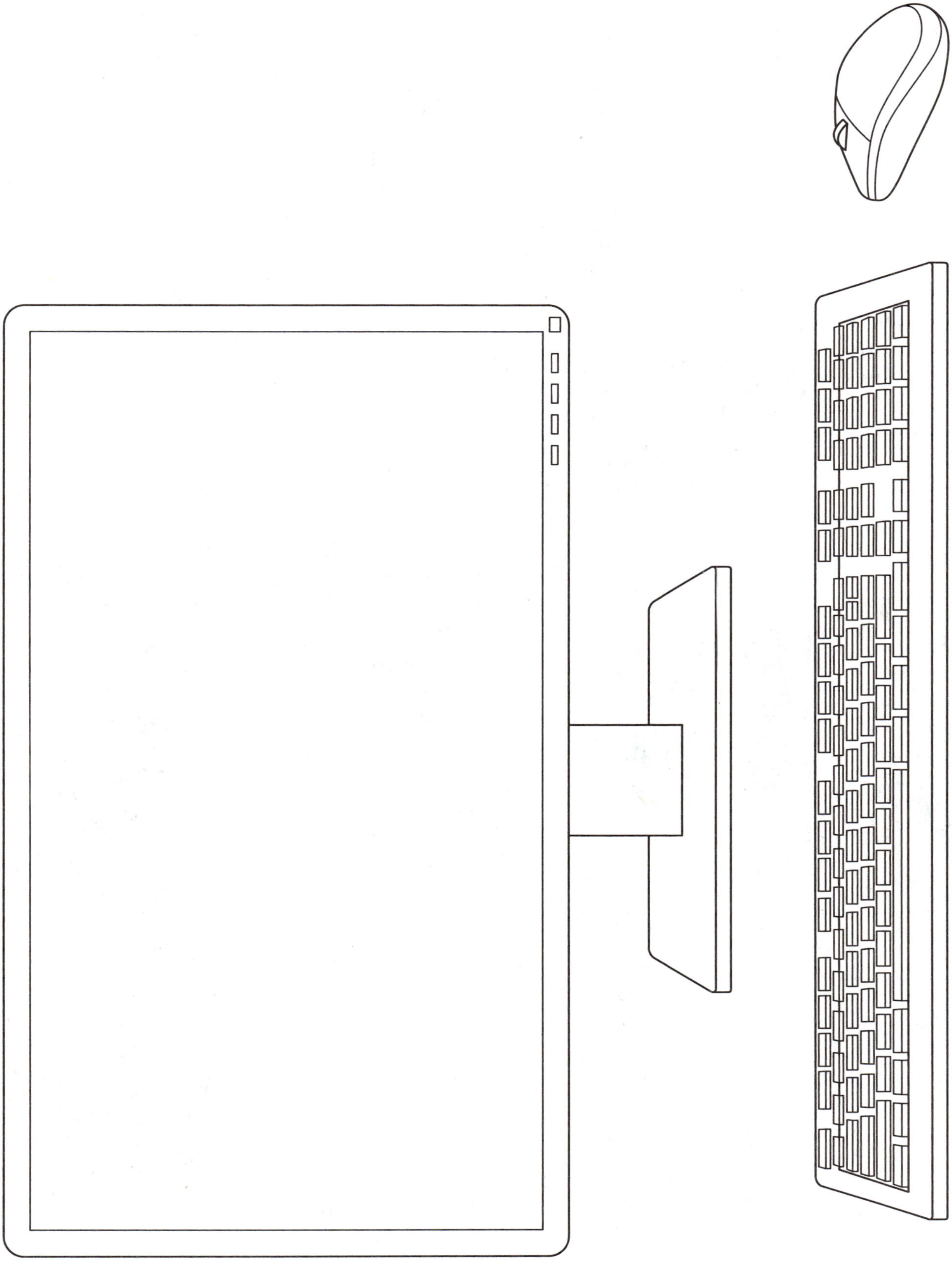

81

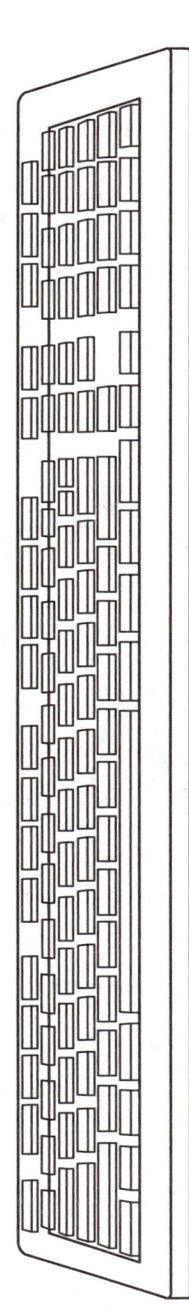

Side 1

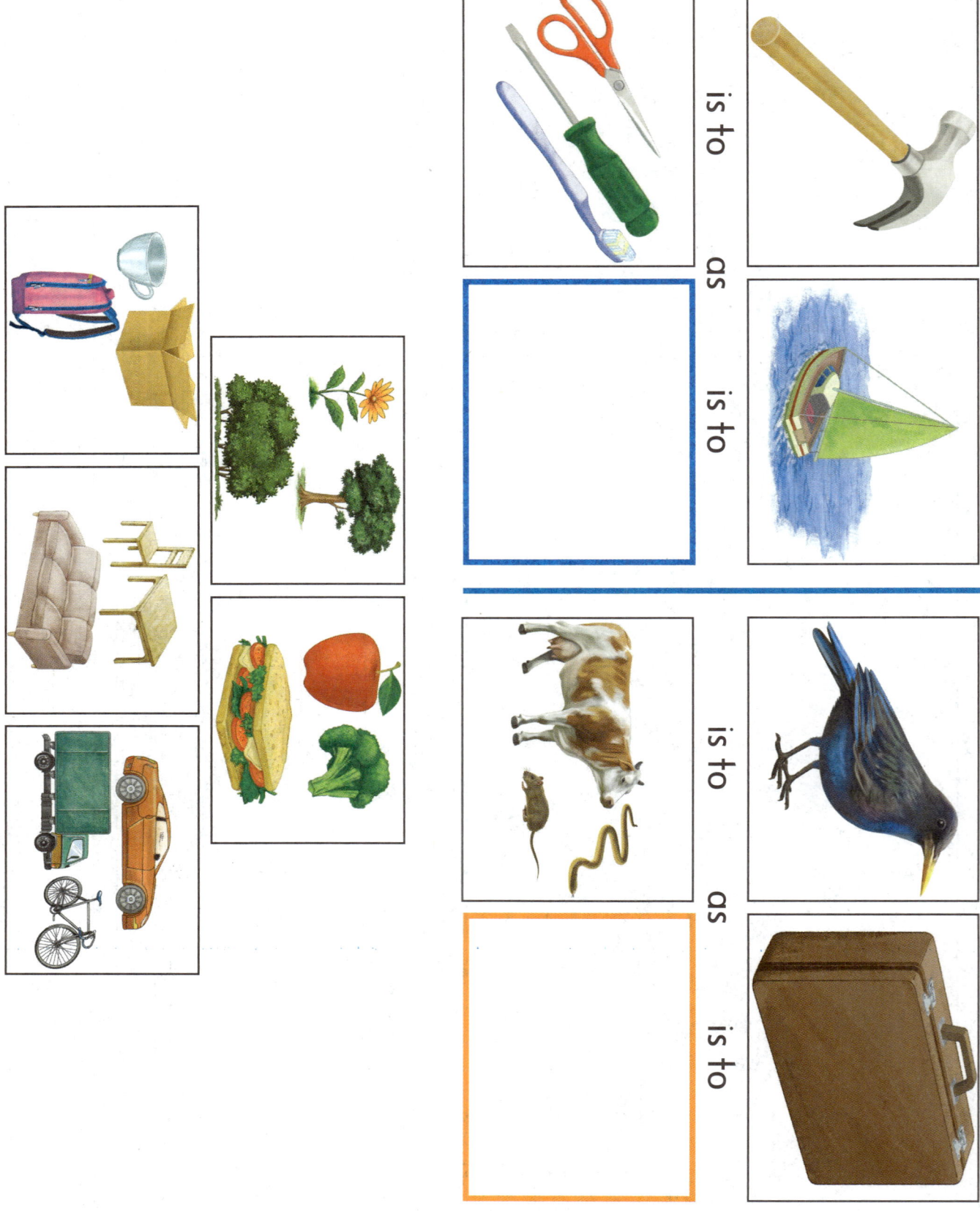

Side 2

Name _____

82

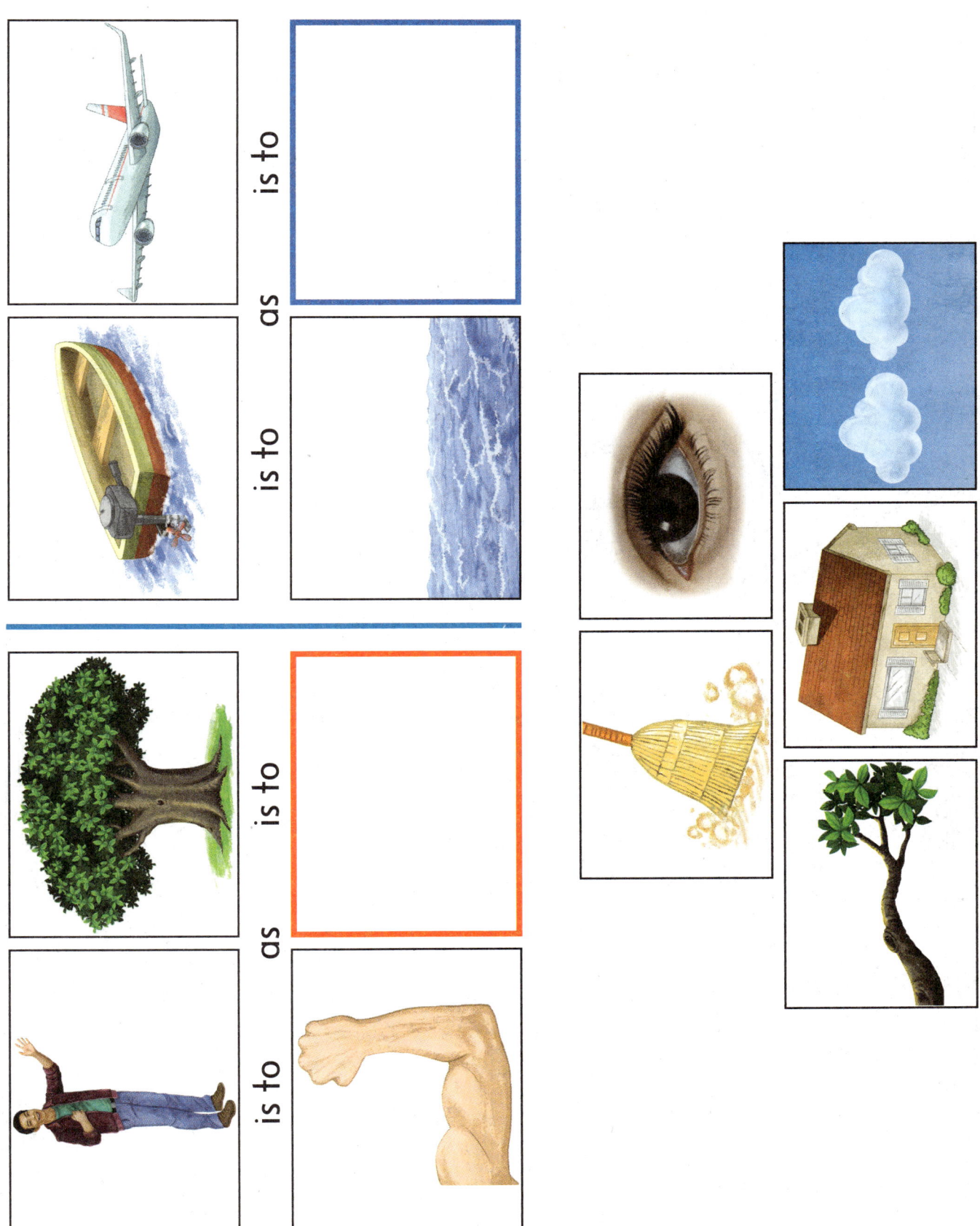

Side 1

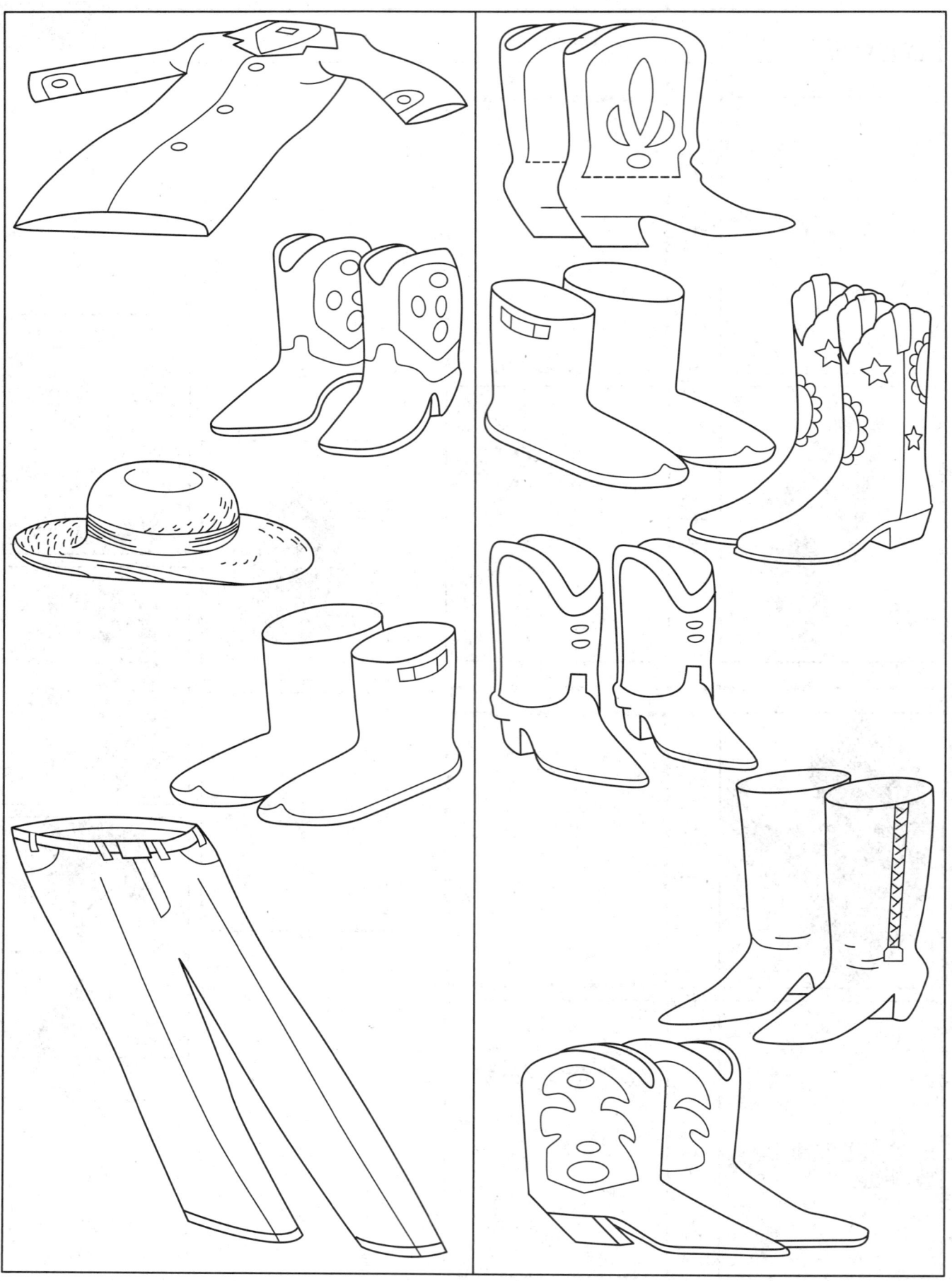

Side 2

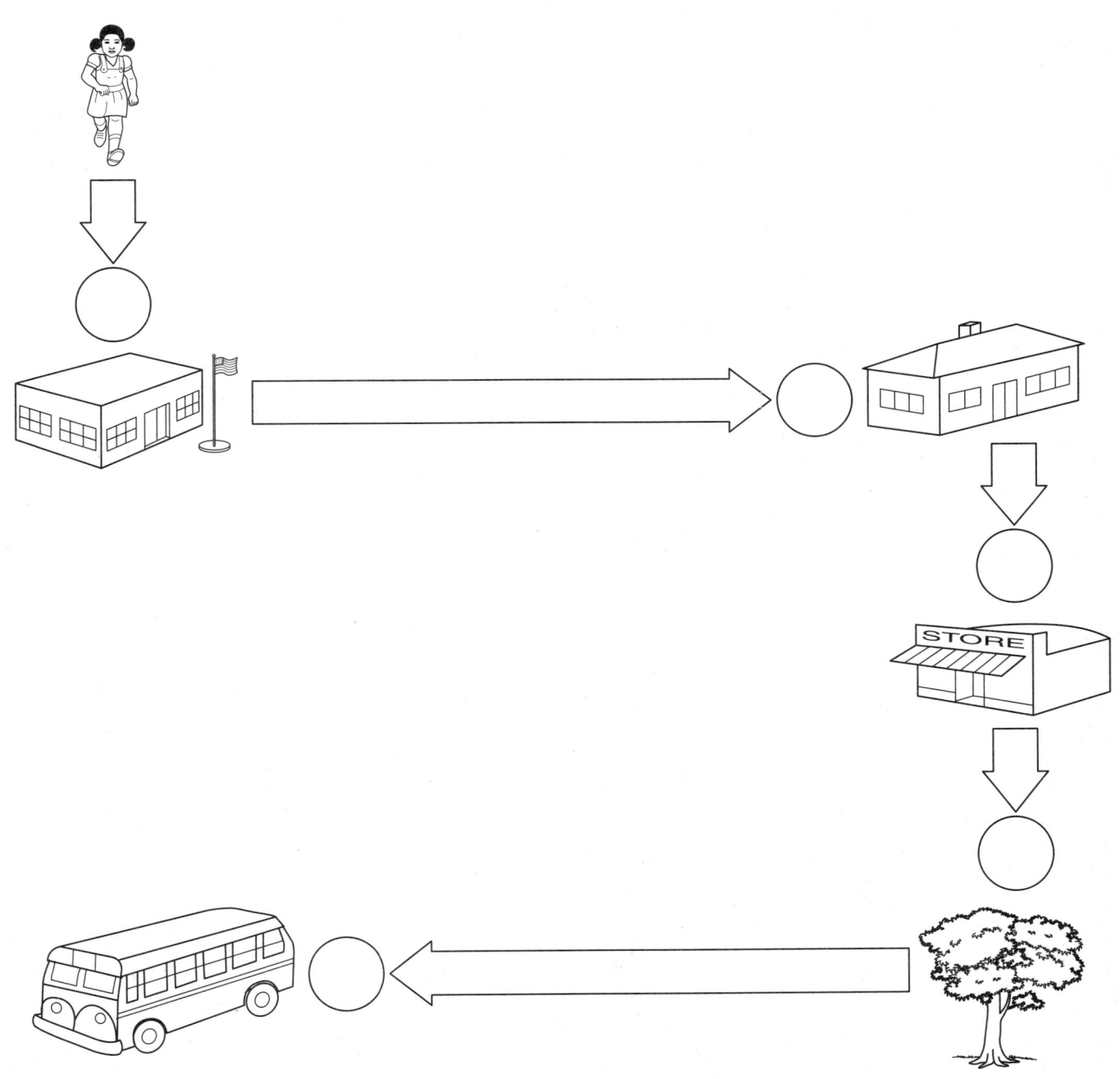

Side 3

Name

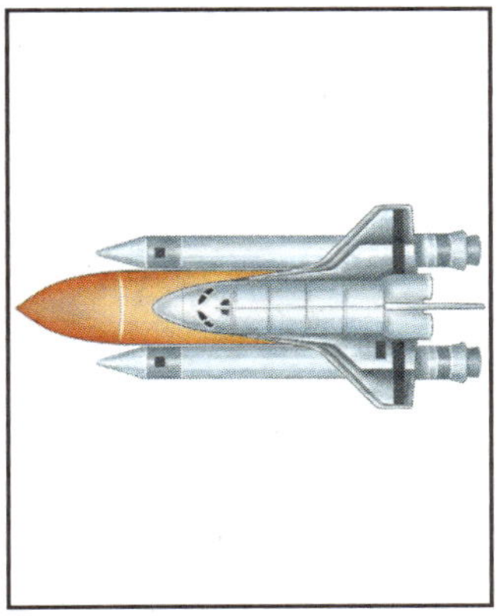

is to

as

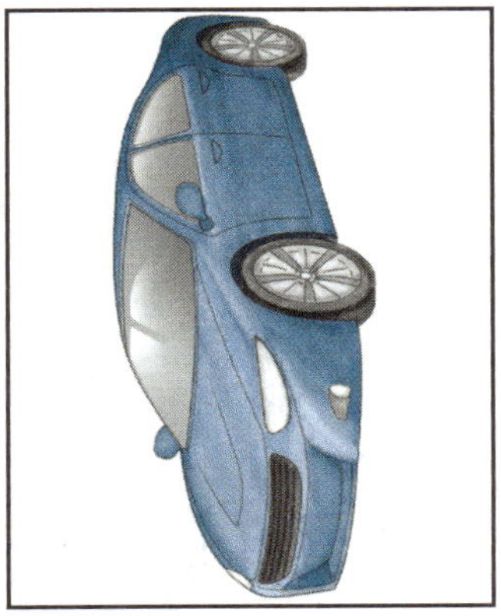

is to

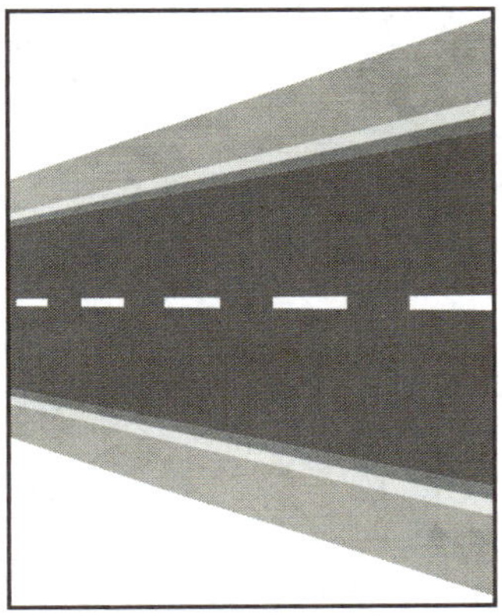

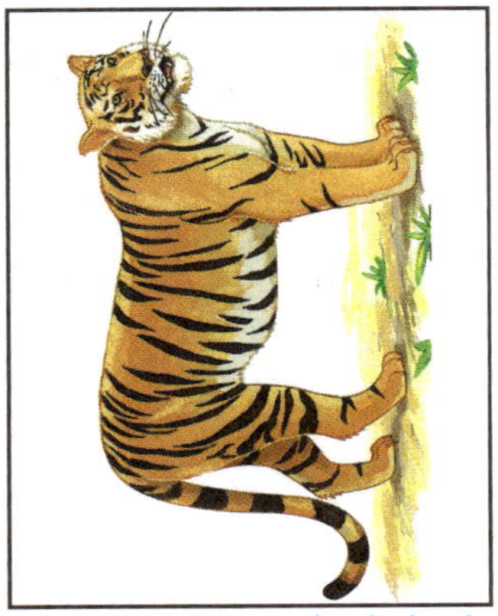

is to

as

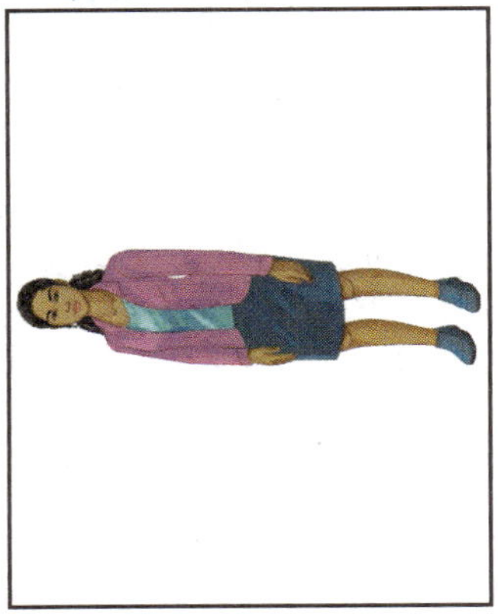

is to

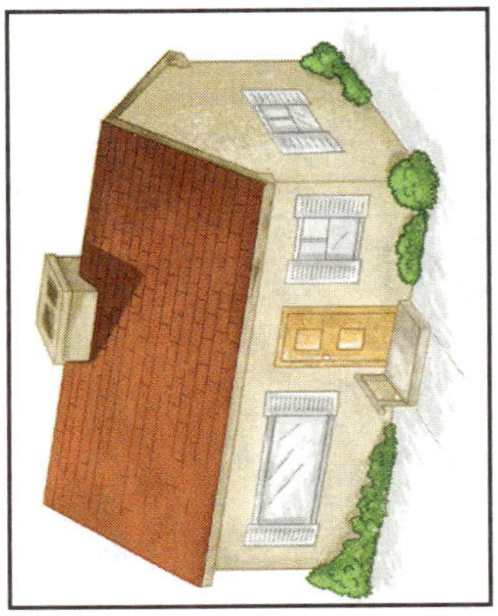

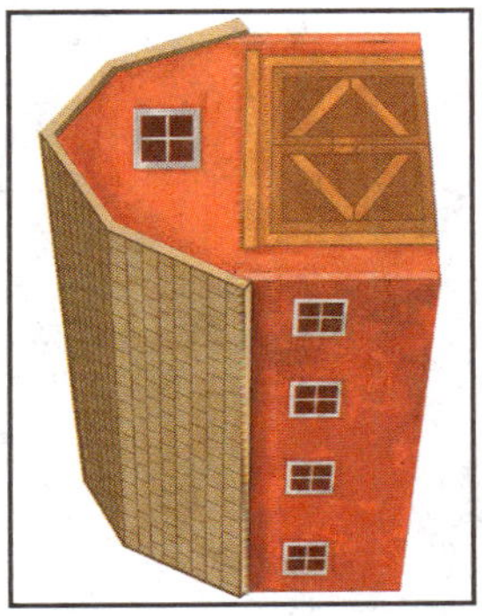

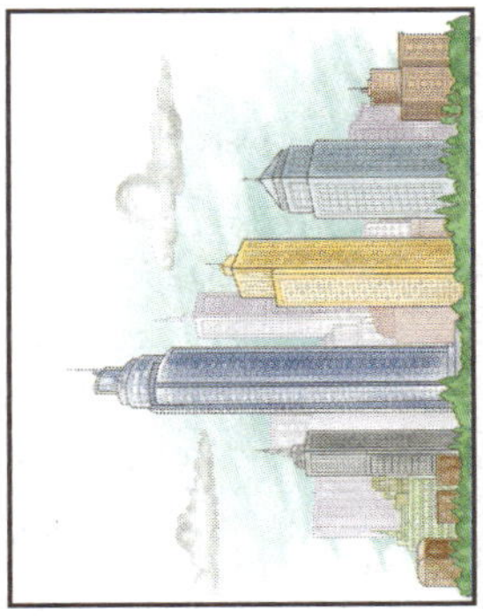

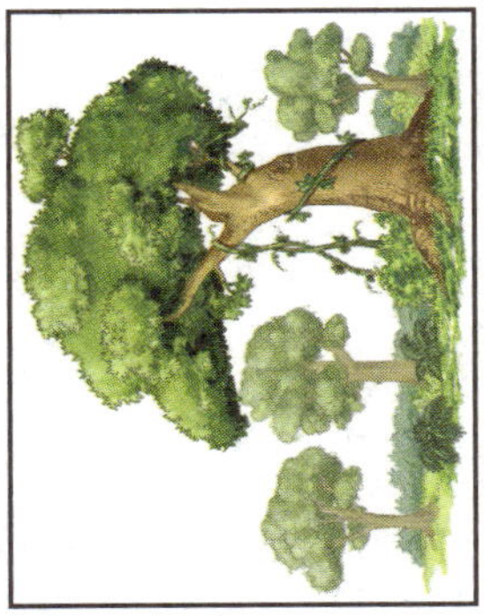

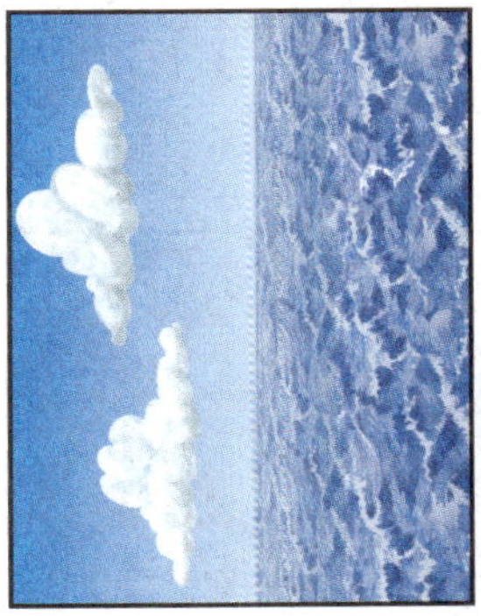

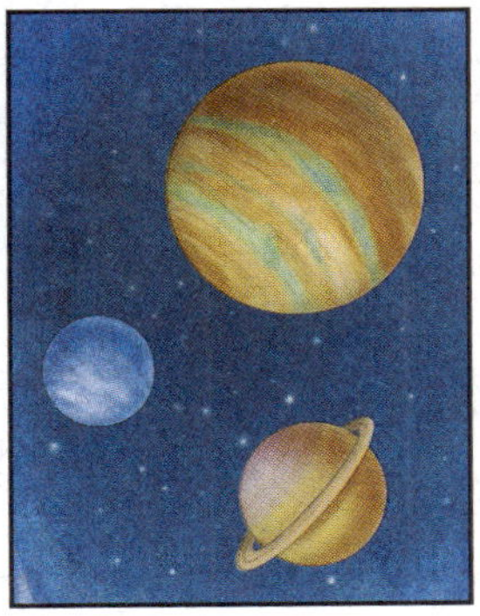

True	False

1. A hammer is a tool. _____

2. You wear shoes on your hands. _____

3. A hat is a building. _____

Side 2

Name

84

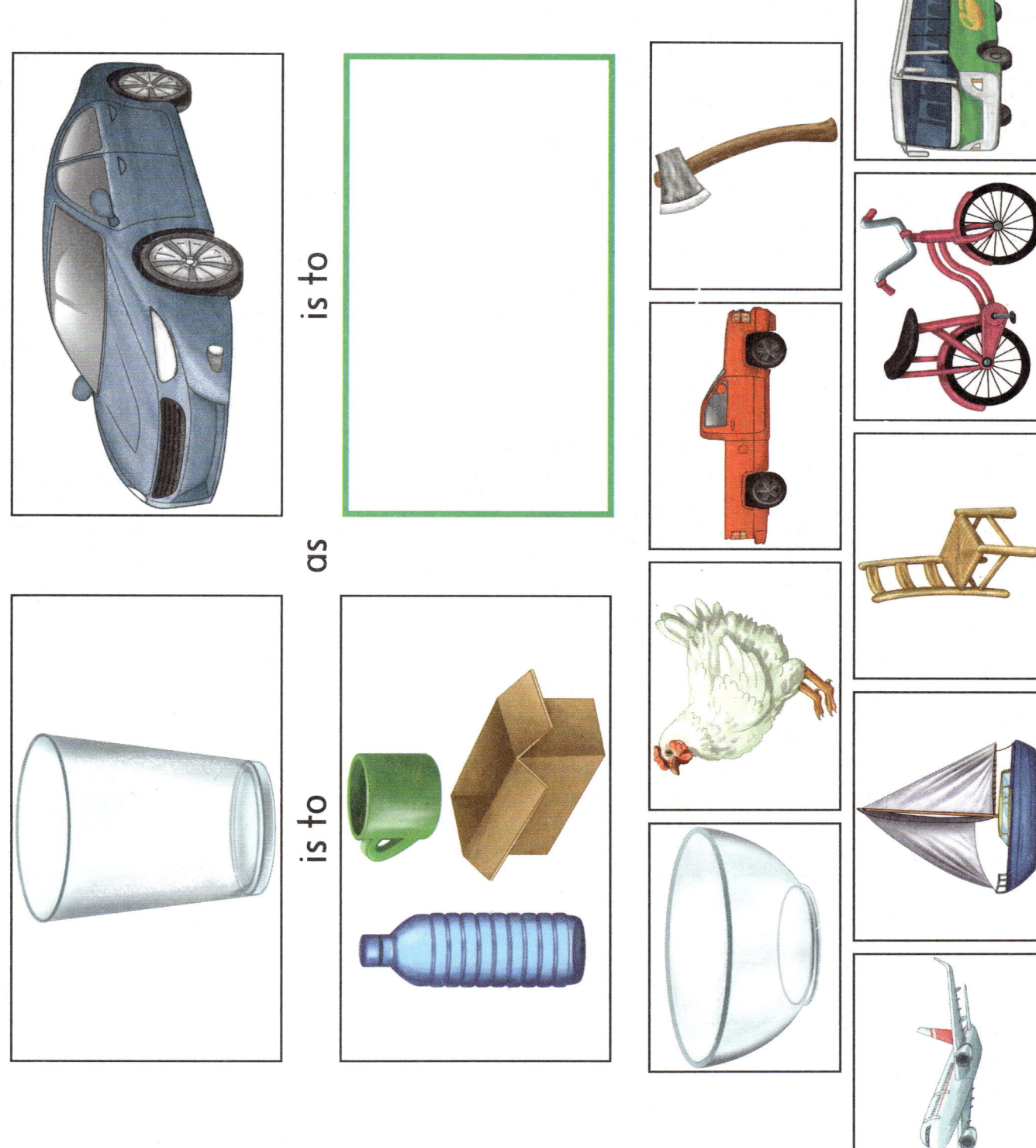

Side 1

winter　　　　spring　　　　summer　　　　fall

Side 2

Name _____

85

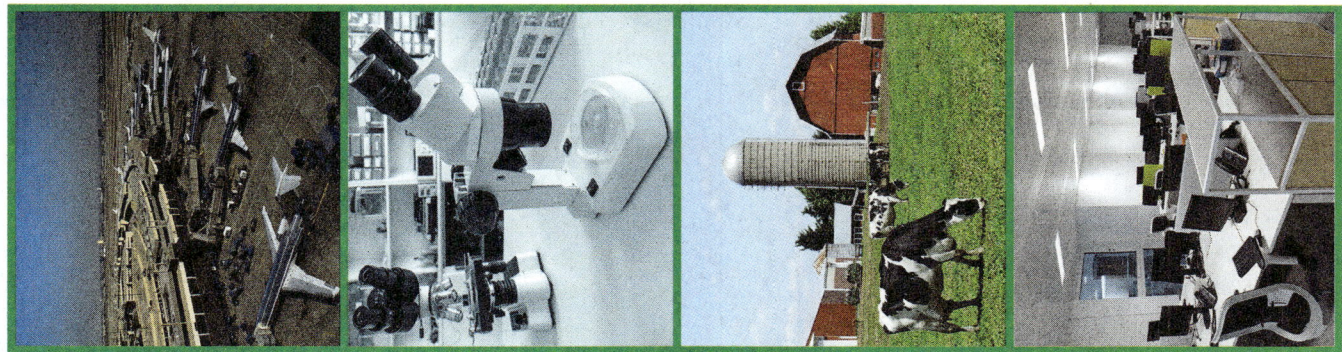

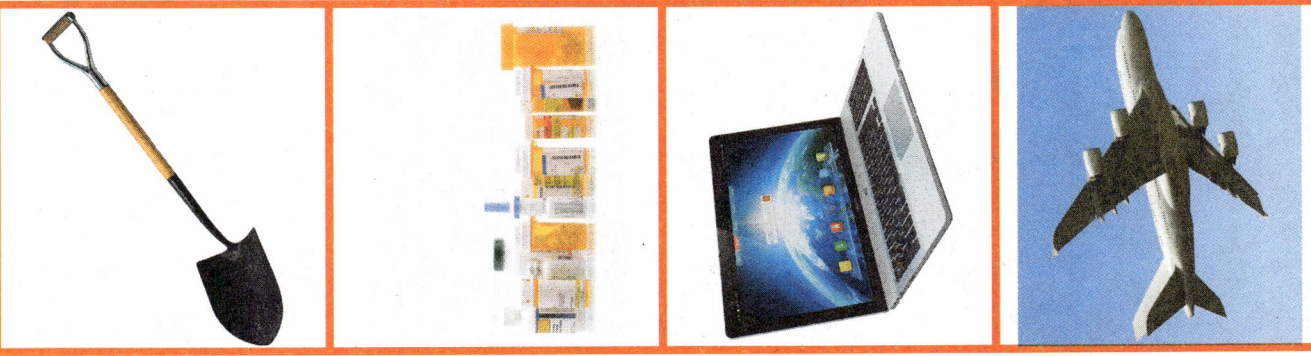

Side 1

food   clothing   animals

nuts _____

coat _____

cat _____

pants _____

goat _____

cake _____

dress _____

shirt _____

Name

 is to  as

 is to

 is to  as

 is to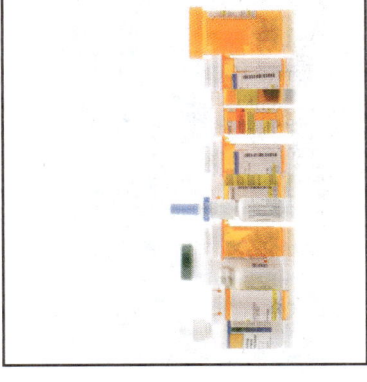

86

Side 1

containers	numbers	tools

jar _____

six _____

saw _____

bag _____

ten _____

rake _____

cup _____

three _____

mop _____

nine _____

Side 2

Name

87

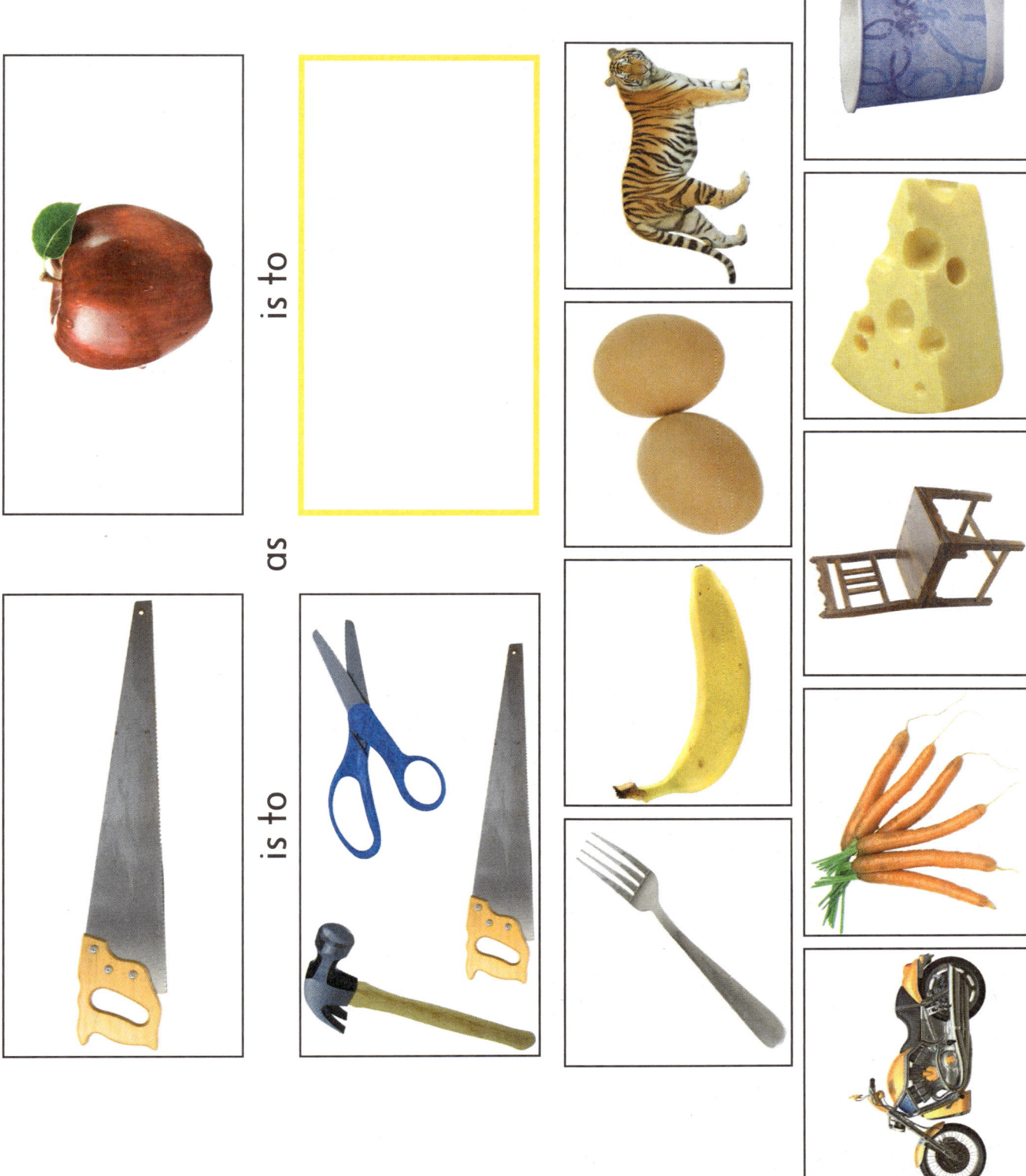

Side 1

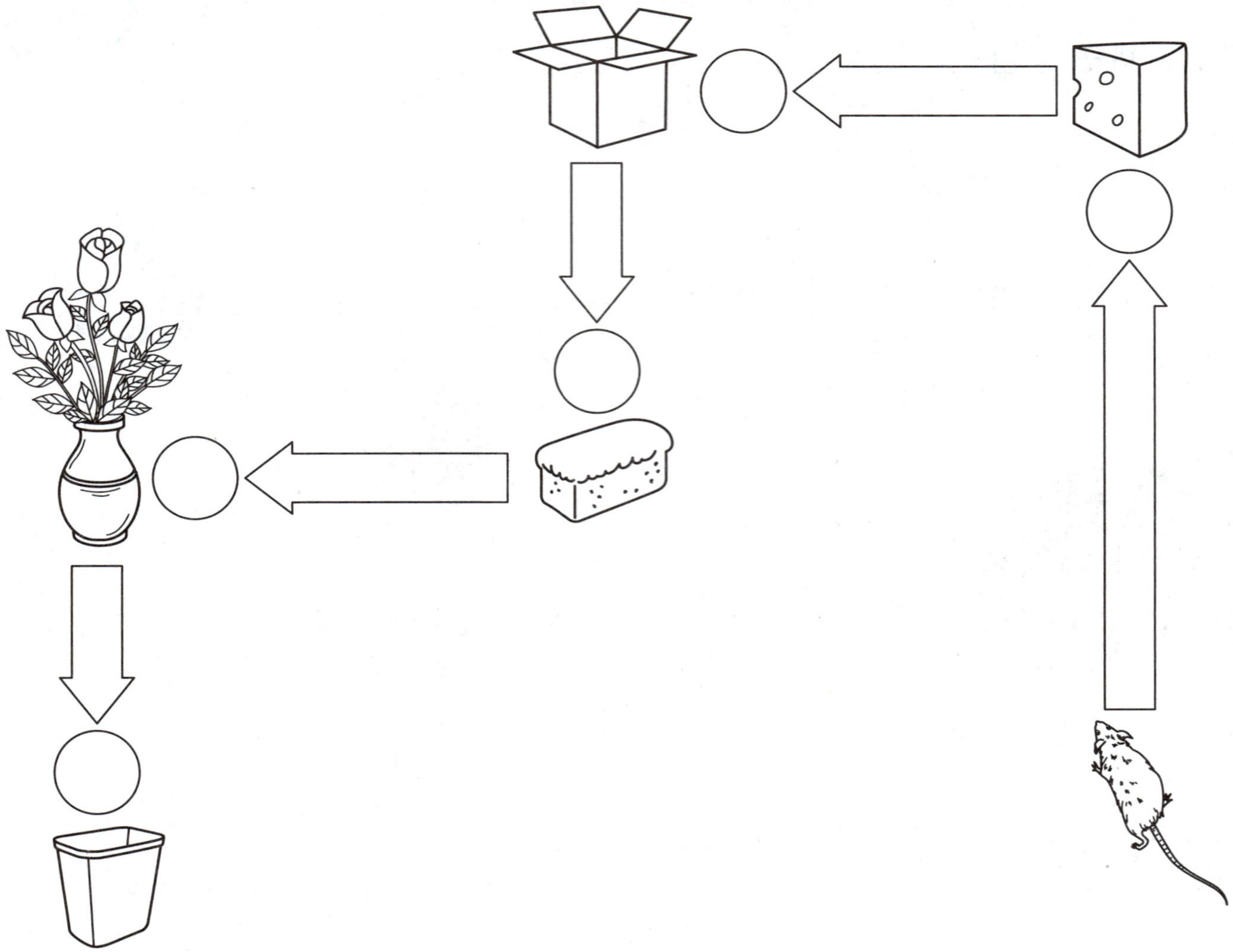

1. james scott and daisy went to pauls house on tuesday

2. will paul come to my house in june or july

3. my sister and i want to play with his dog

Side 2

Name _____

| early | cry | start | easy | throw | slow |

1. The girls were late to school.
   _____
   _____

2. When will he finish his dinner?
   _____
   _____

3. My brother can catch a ball.
   _____
   _____

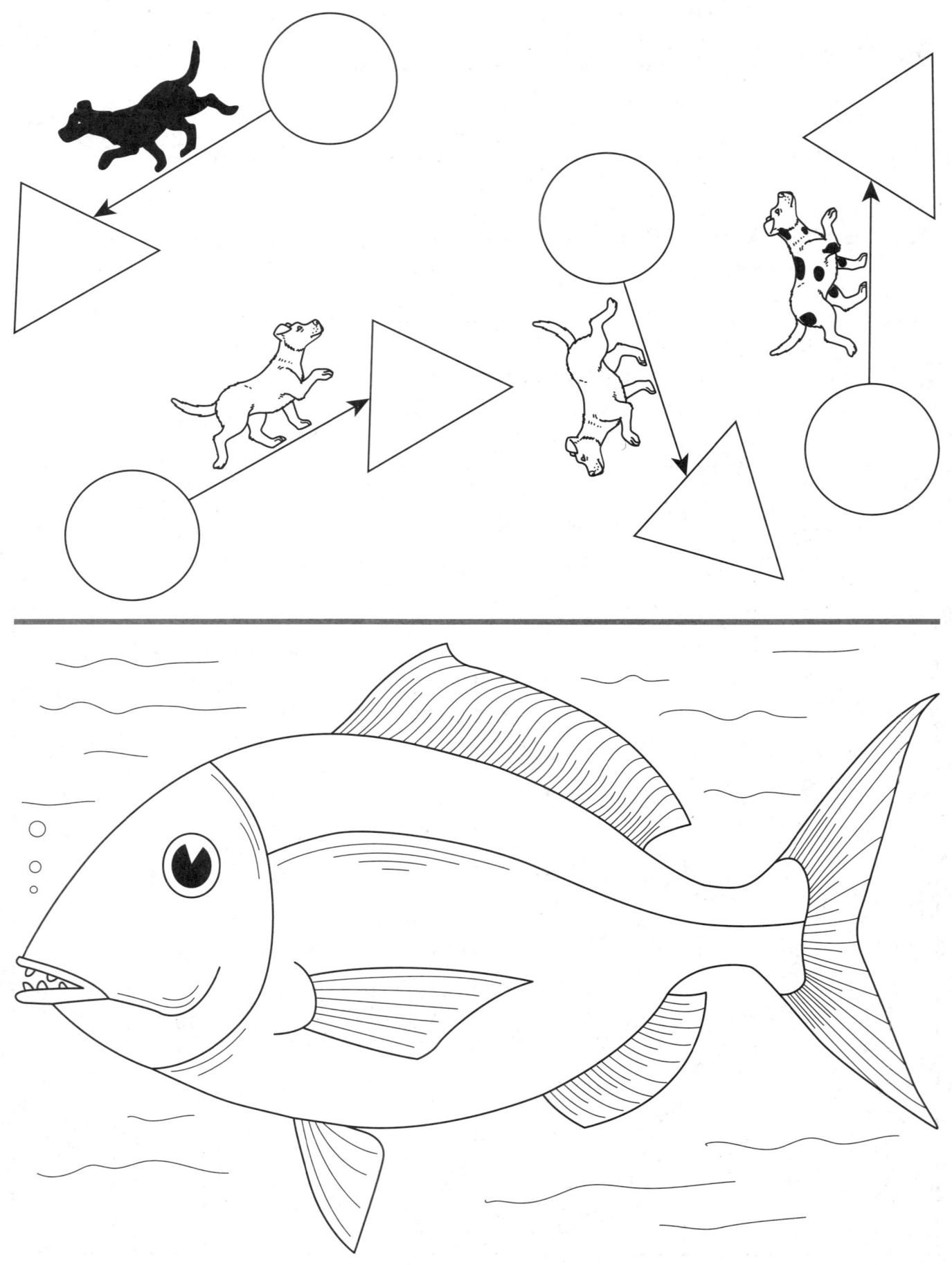

Side 2

Name

89

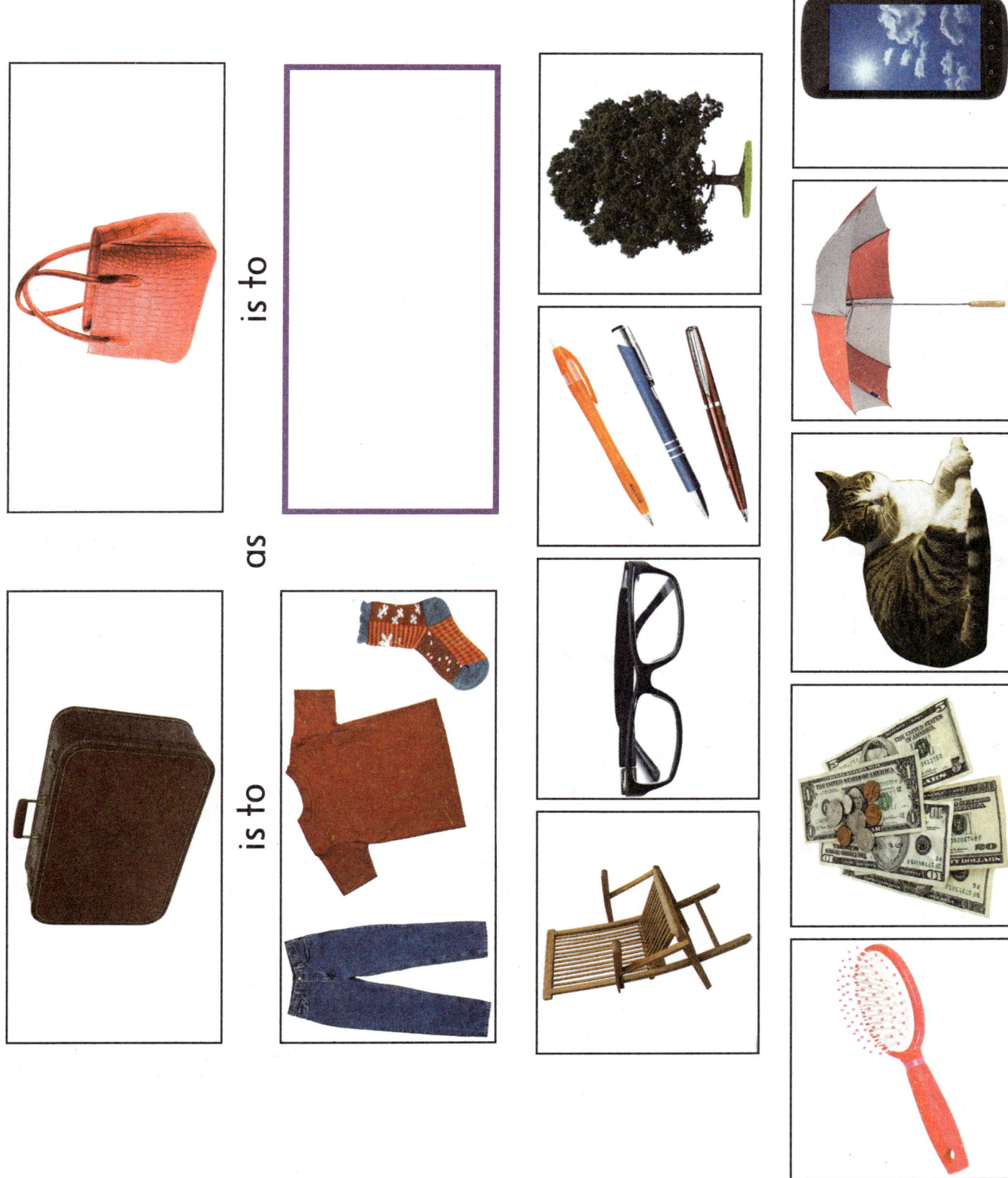

Side 1

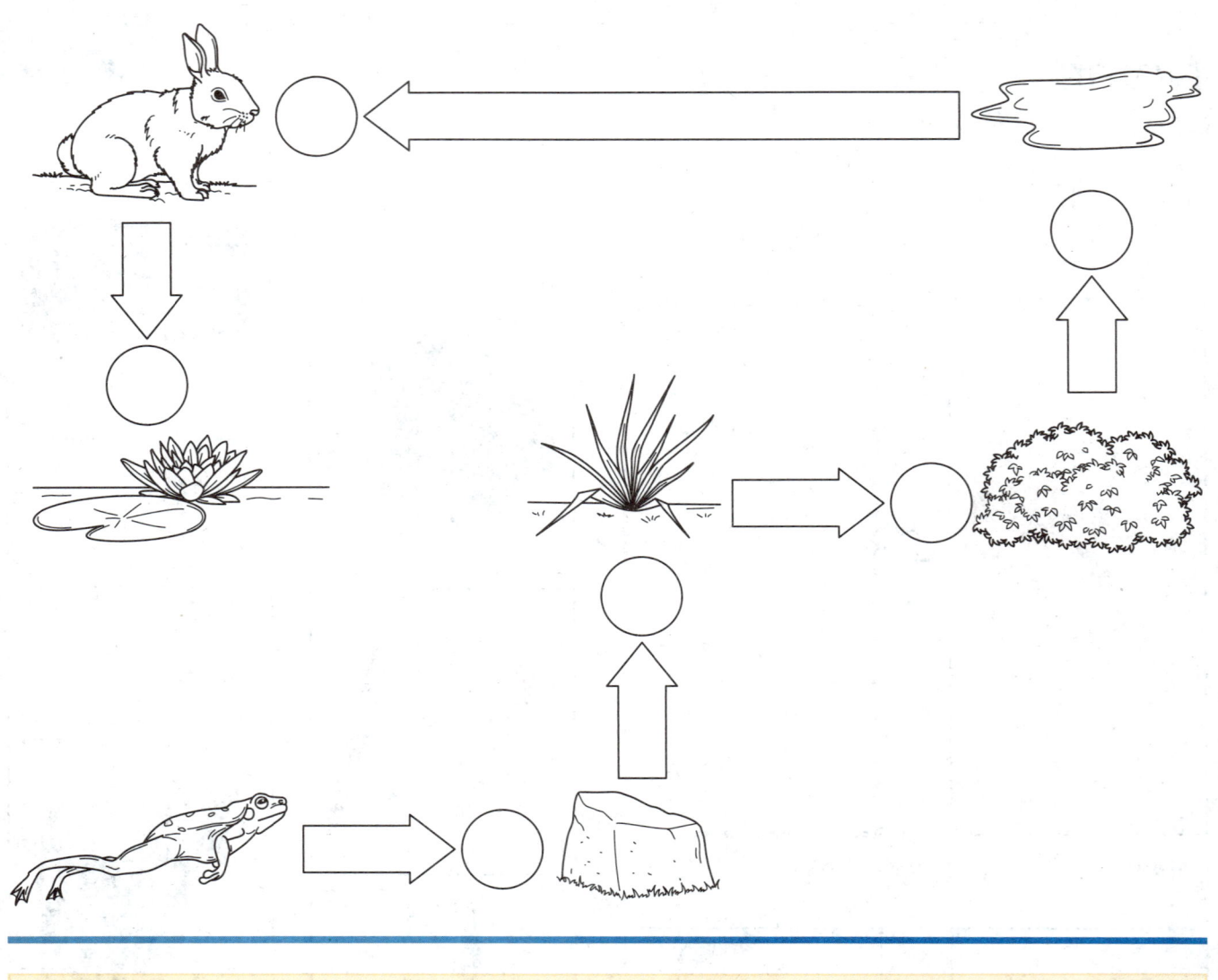

| finish | hard | well | start | noisy | large |

1. When will this movie end?
_____
_____

2. The patient is healthy.
_____
_____

3. A loud dog was barking.
_____
_____

Side 2

Name _____

| vehicles | animals | clothing |

sock _____   turtle _____

boat _____   tractor _____

shark _____ horse _____

hat _____   dress _____

train _____ car _____

Side 1

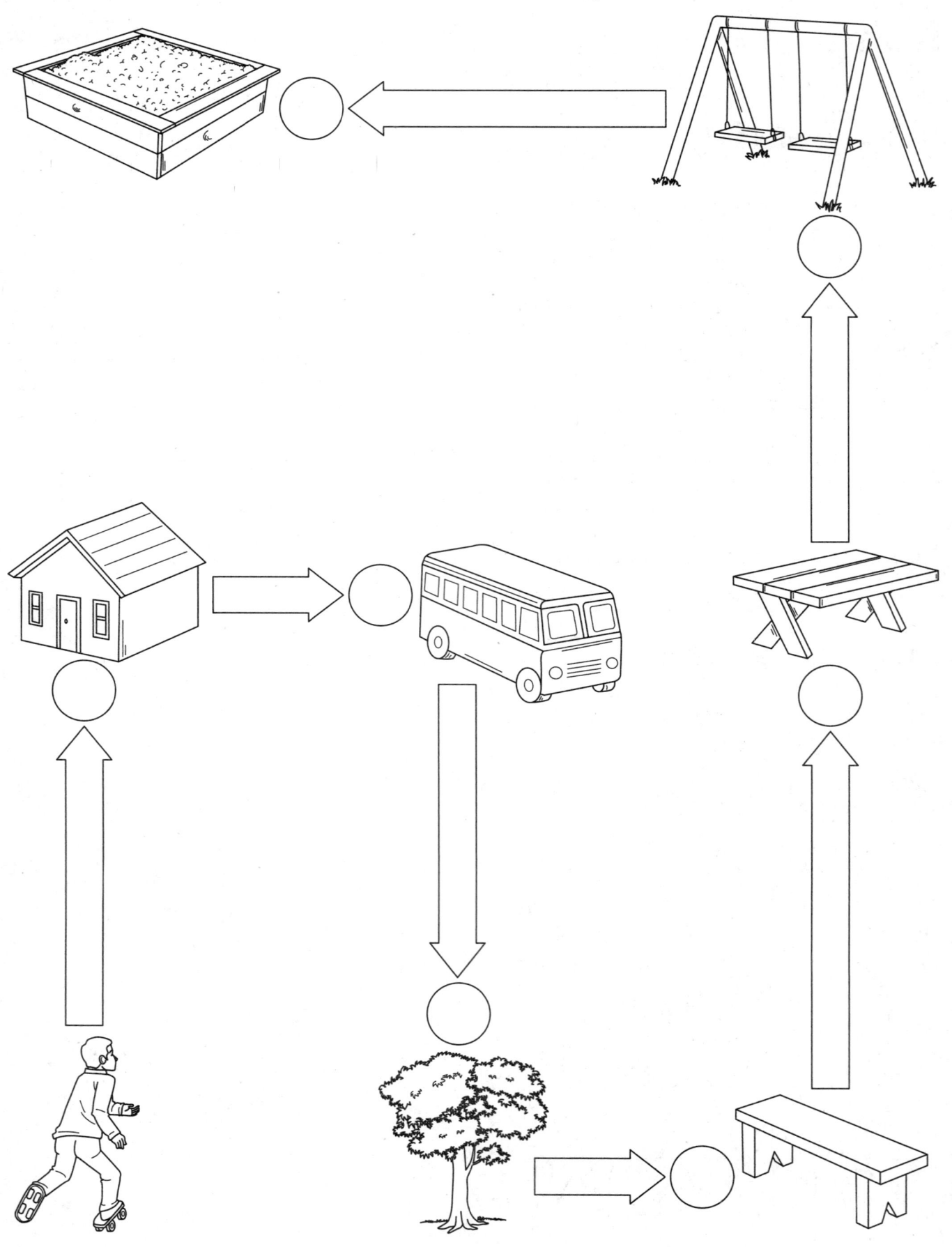

Side 2

Name _____

| ring | gold | cake | medicine | skates |
| necklace | | shoes | food | dress |

1. Hans made a _____ for Hilda.

2. Hilda gave Hans a piece of _____.

3. His papa needed _____.

4. Hans needed _____.

5. I think Hans should buy _____.

Side 1

Side 2

Name _____

92

is to _____ as

is to _____

is to _____ as

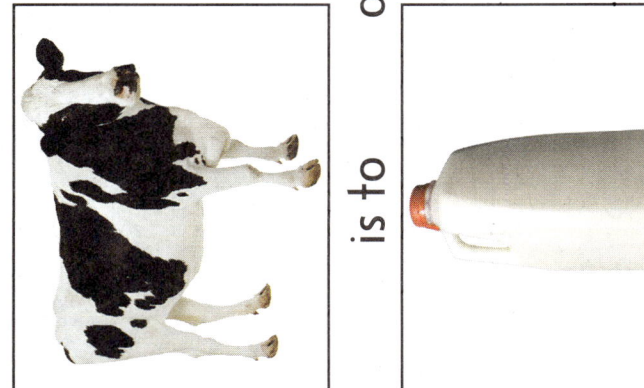
is to _____

Side 1

Side 2

| dog | chewed | bone |

A cat climbed a tree.

Name _____

| plants | containers | food |

bush _____   tree _____

banana _____   suitcase _____

box _____   flower _____

cup _____   soup _____

bread _____   eggs _____

1. ann and i will see the movie on tuesday

2. will you be here in january february or march

3. mike s team won both games

Side 1

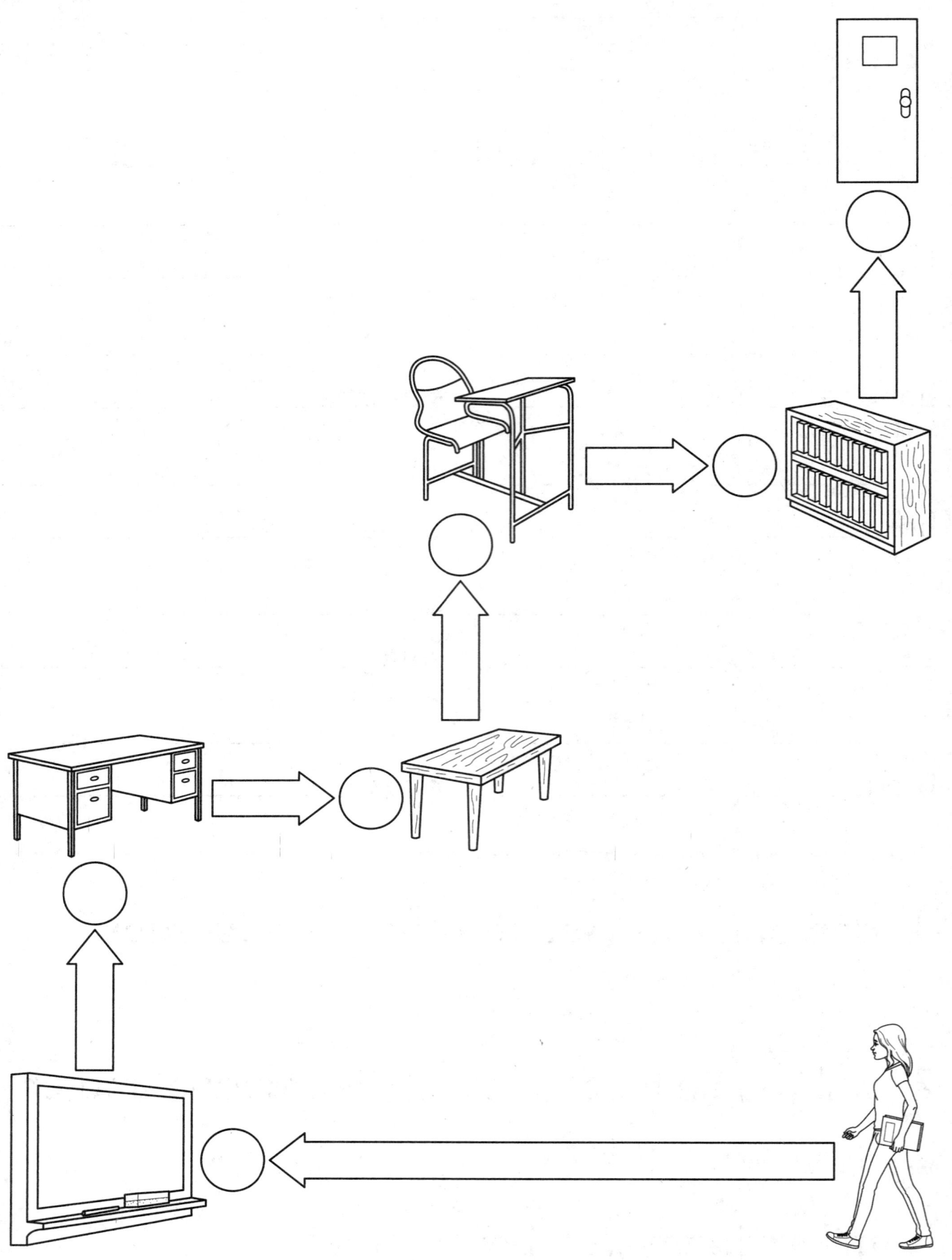

Side 2

Name _____

94

 is to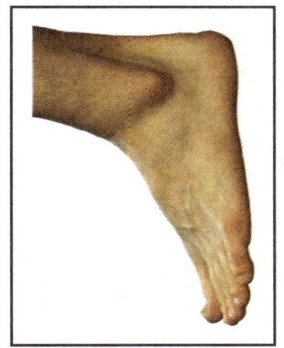

 is to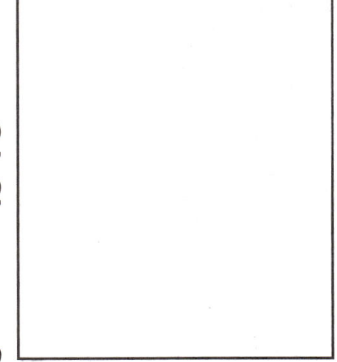

as

 is to

Side 1

True   False

1. A doll is a tool. _____

2. Dogs have wings. _____

3. A hammer is a tool. _____

Side 2

Name _____

95

Side 1

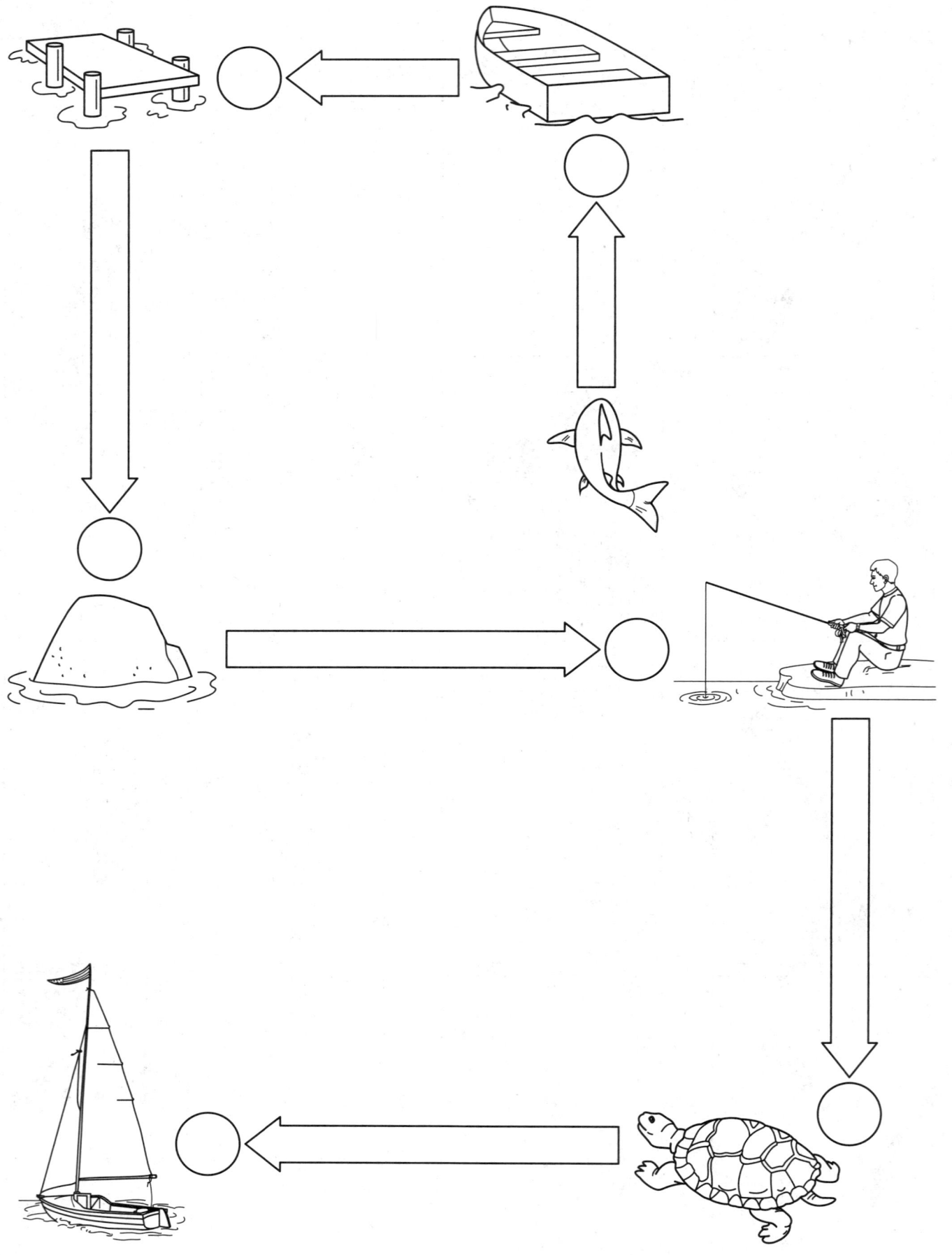

Side 2

Name _____   96

Hans   Papa   Gretel   Mama
_____   _____   _____   _____

Hilda   Dr. Bookman   Karl
_____   _____   _____

_____ bought skates after Papa got medicine. ☐

_____ won the race after falling down. ☐

_____ bought a necklace before the race. ☐

_____ told Mama to pay him later. ☐

_____ was in the lead at the first curve. ☐

My favorite character is _____.

Side 1

Side 2

Name _____

tuesday march 14 2019

friday april 8 2004

saturday december 23 1914

monday february 20 804

friday january 7 2019

sunday august 1 1535

Today is _____ .

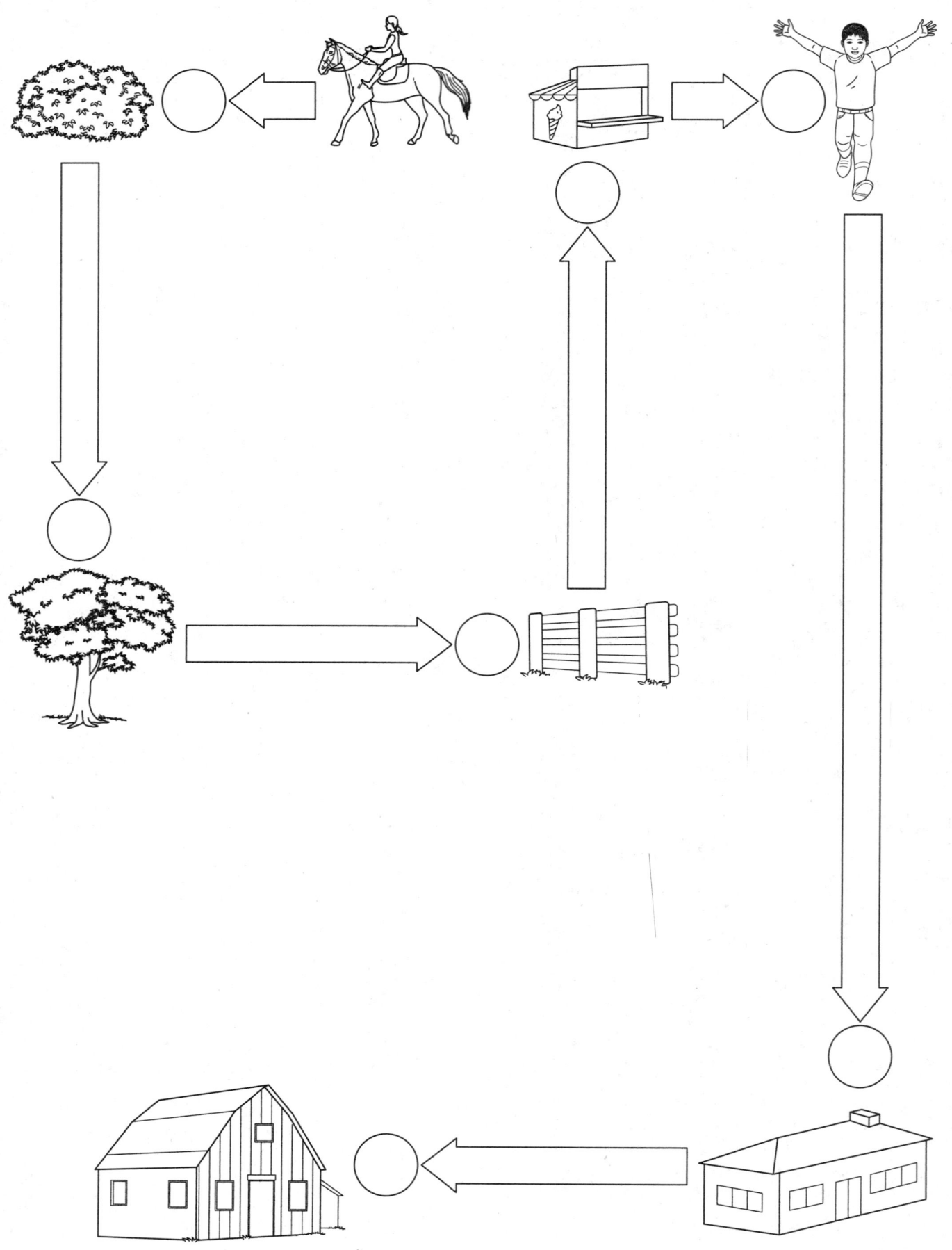

Side 2

Name _____

1. i was born on friday october 11 2012

2. bob and jen will go on april 13

3. december and january are the coldest months

Today is _____ .

| sad | fast | happy | cold | slow | hot |

1. She is a happy kitty.

_____

2. Jim is a fast runner.

_____

3. Hot water is in the sink.

_____

Side 1

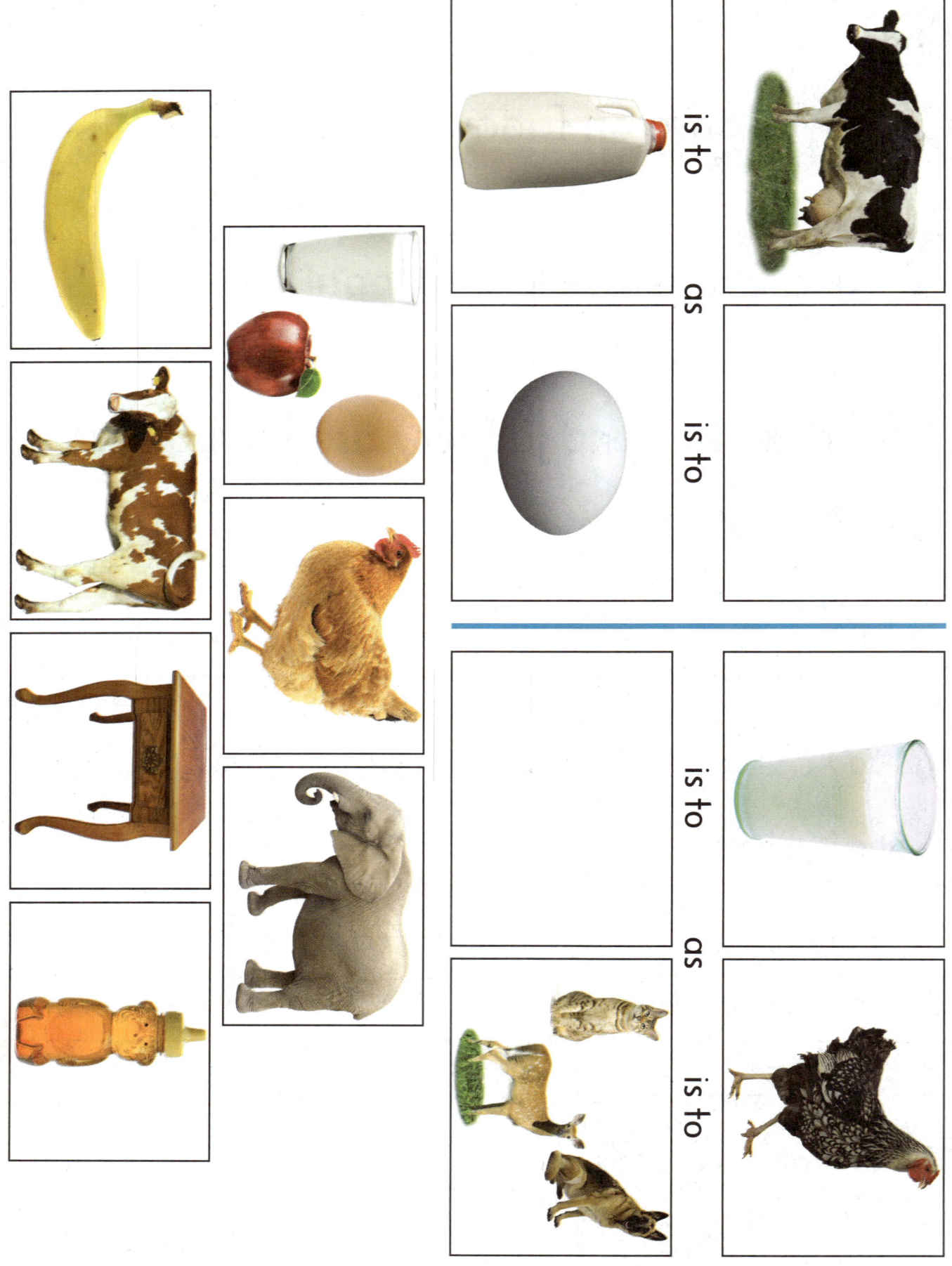

Side 2

Name _____

1. can we meet on wednesday march 12

2. you will be gone in april may and june

3. my birthday is february 19 1992

Today is _____ .

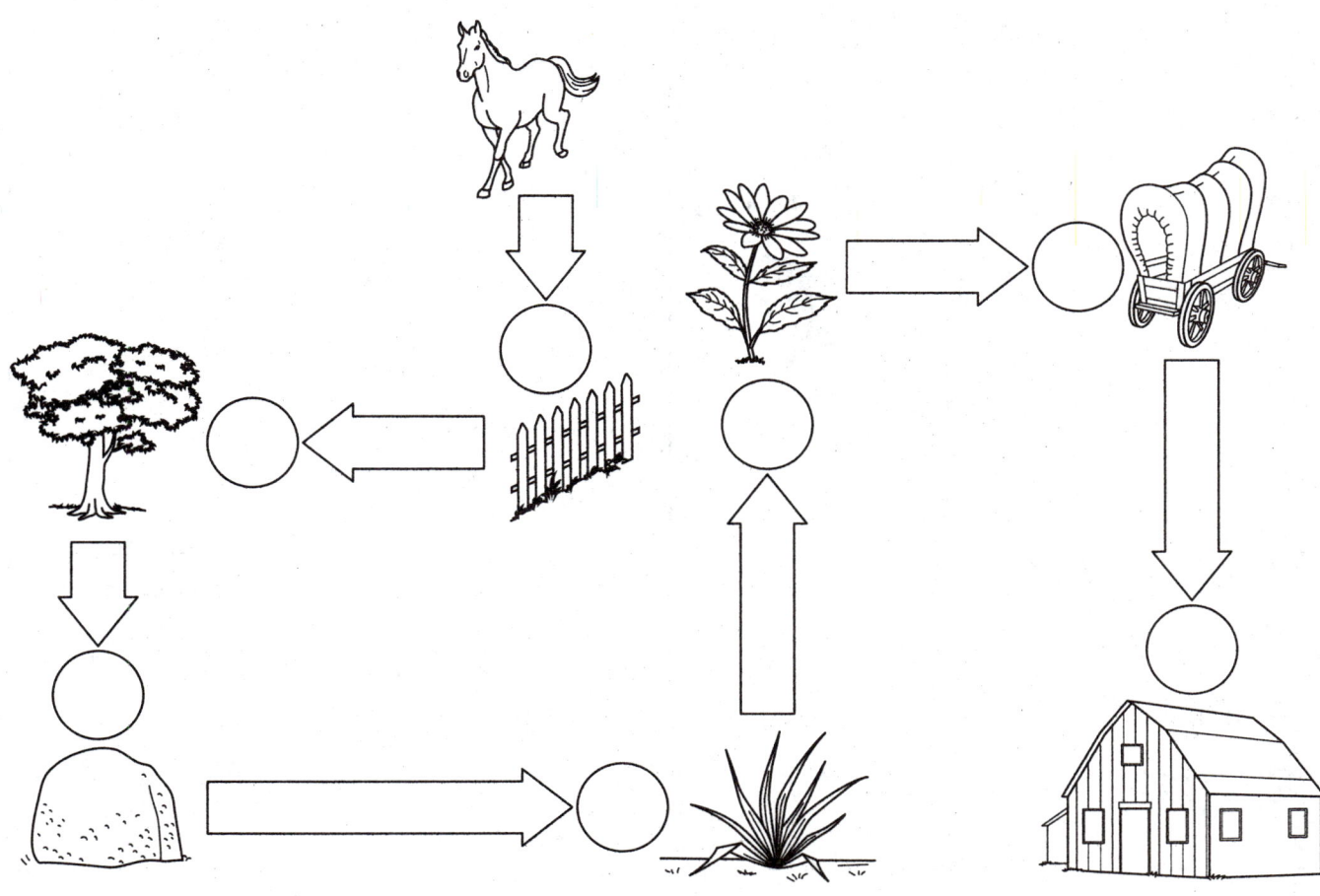

Side 1

Side 2

Name _____

100

is to ___ as ___ is to ___

are to ___ as ___ are to ___

Side 1

tools	plants	animals

hammer _____   grass _____

flower _____   tree _____

lion _____   screwdriver _____

dog _____   ax _____

shovel _____   fish _____

Side 2

Name

101

Side 1

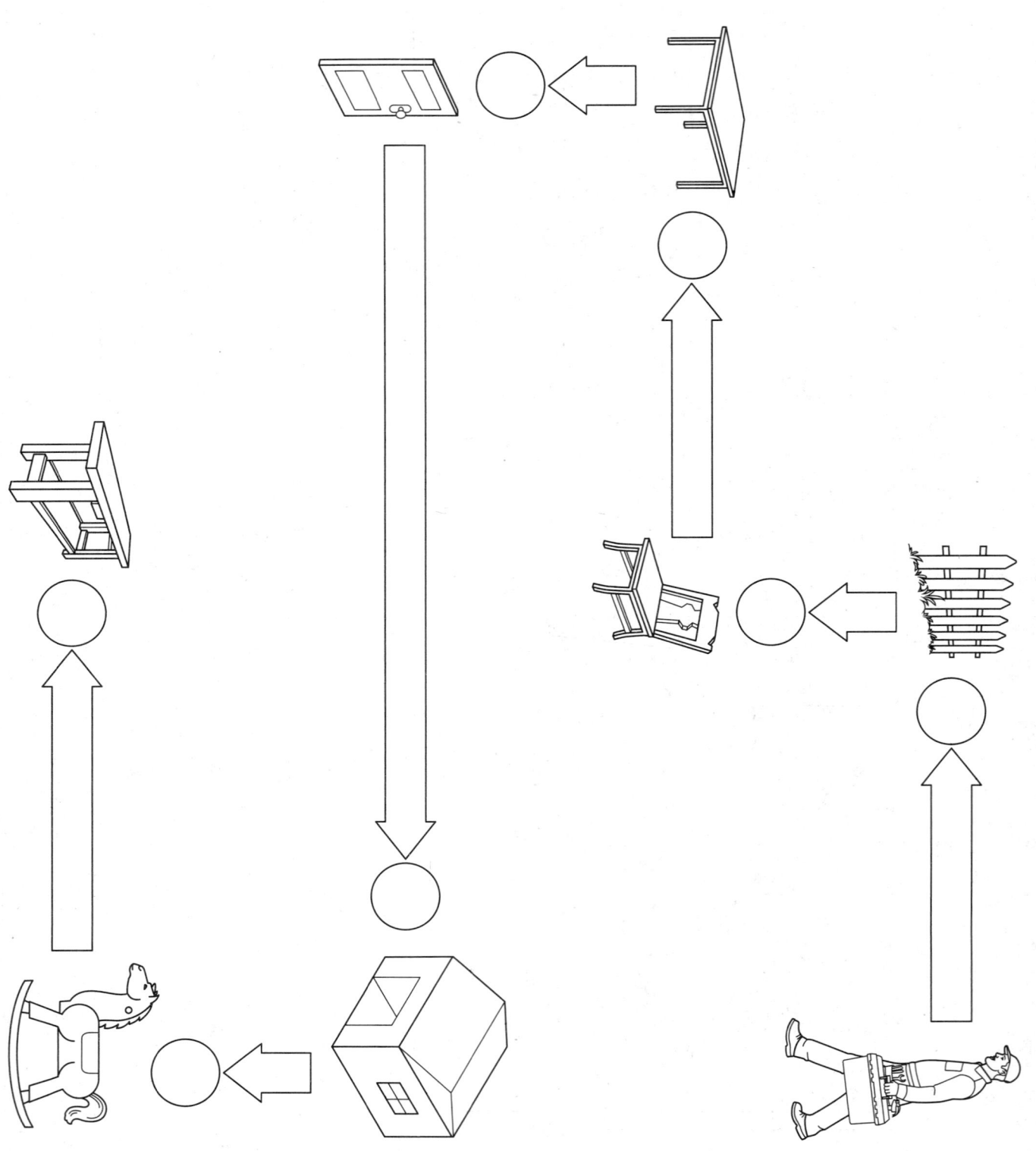

Side 2

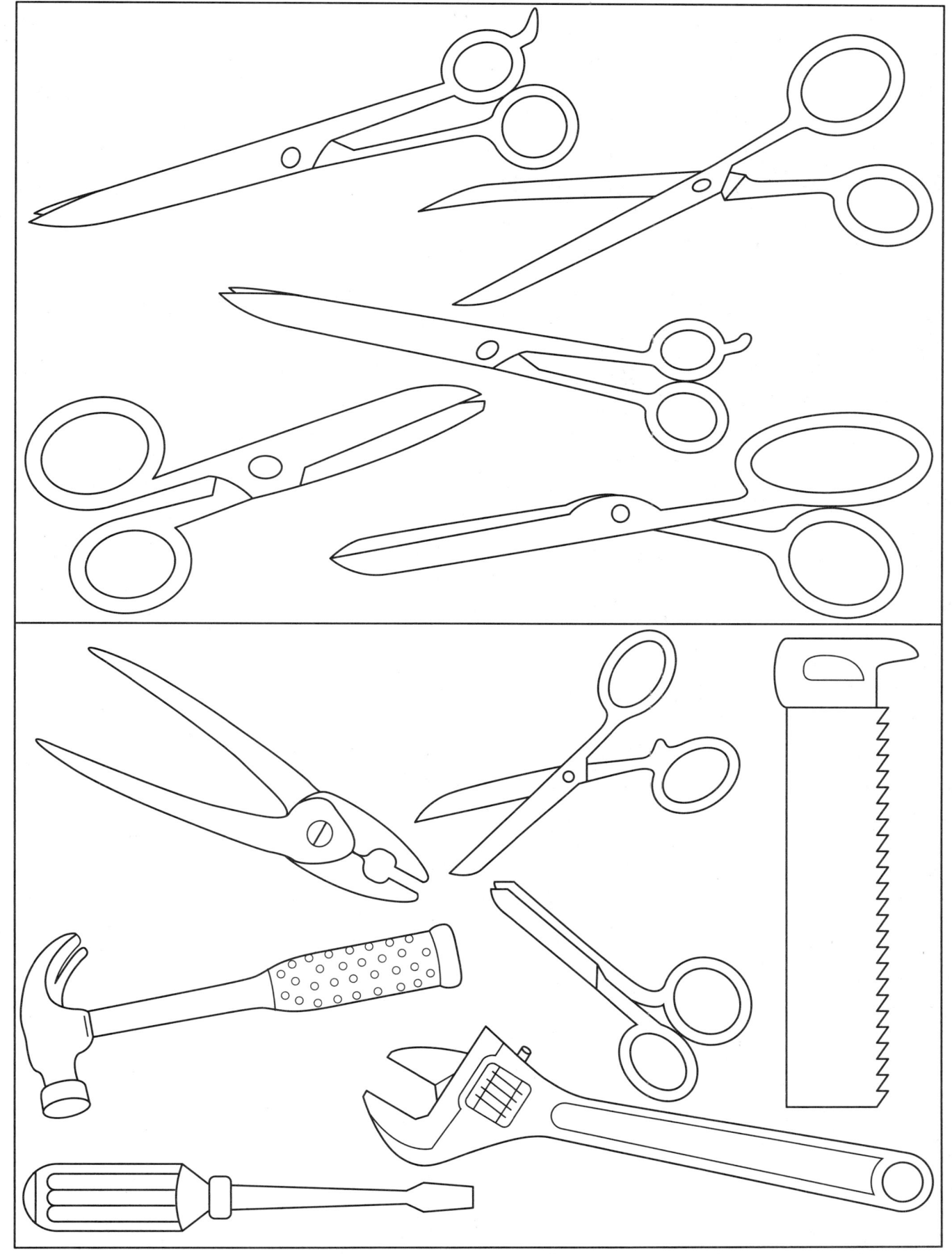

Name _____

Today is _____ .

1. president lincoln was born on wednesday february 12 1809

2. mary gary and jerry will go on tuesday or thursday

3. am i going to sams house

| full | empty | big | small | long | short |

1. The big bike is mine.
   _____

2. She had a long pencil.
   _____

3. His cup is full.
   _____

Side 1

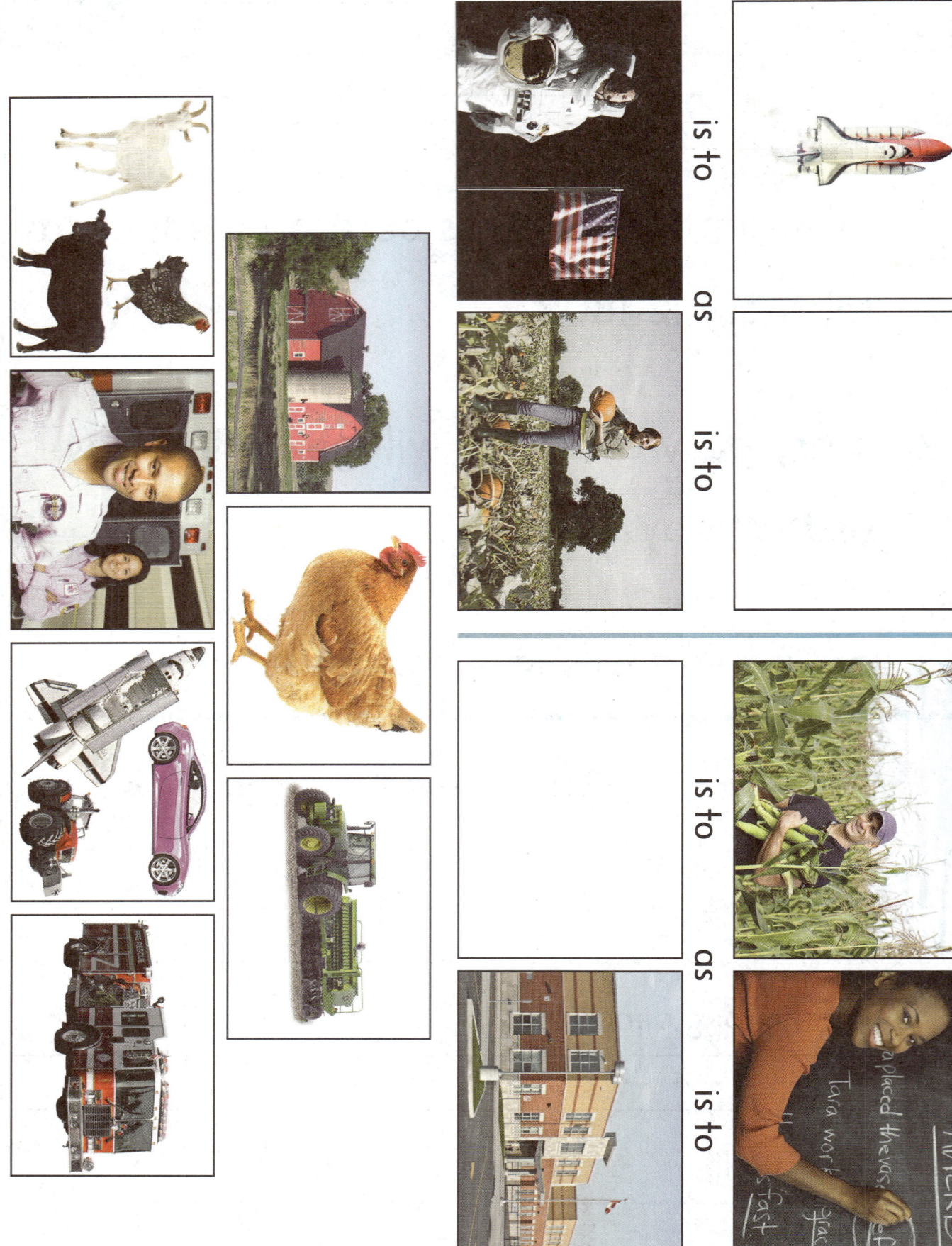

Name

103

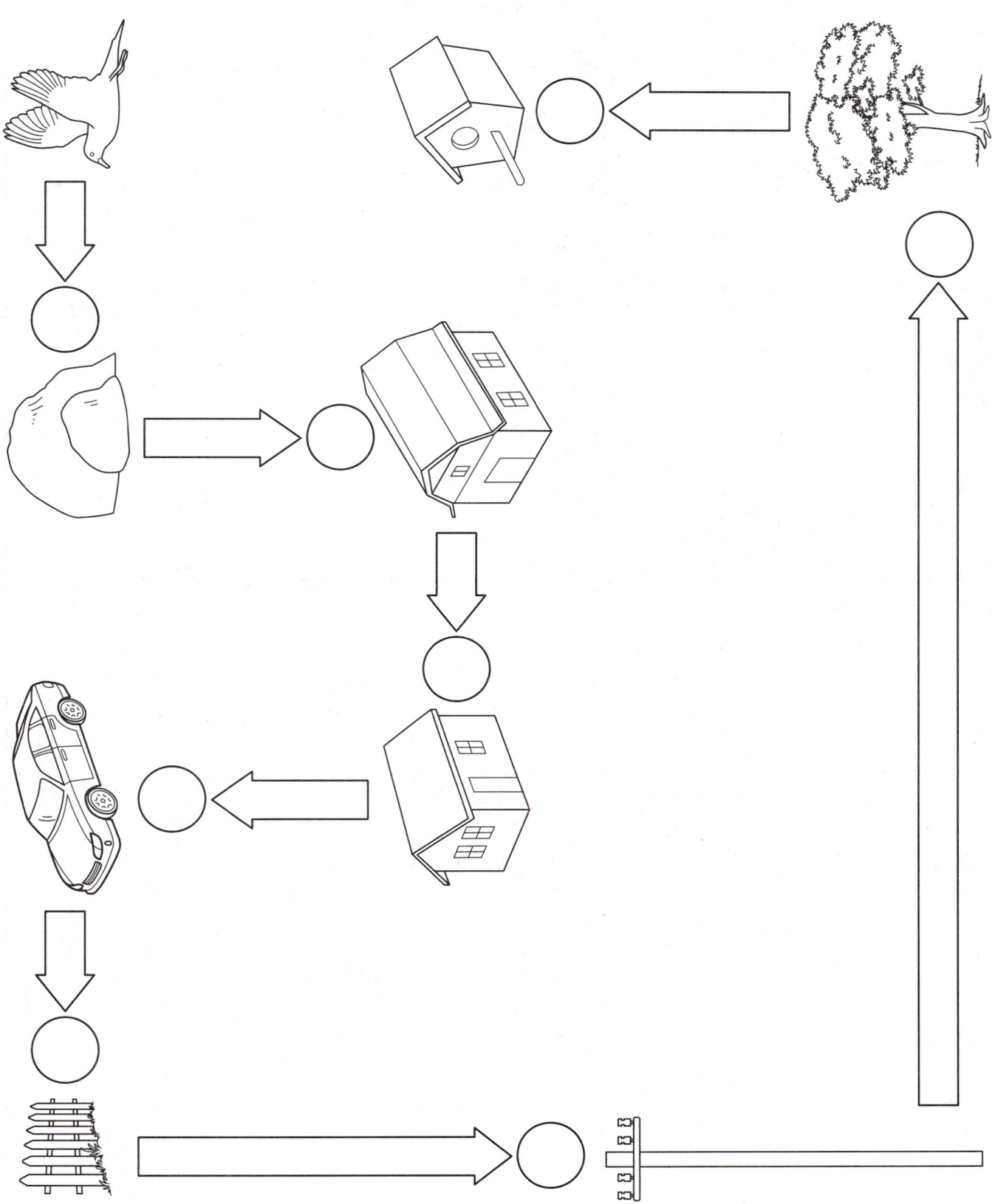

Side 1

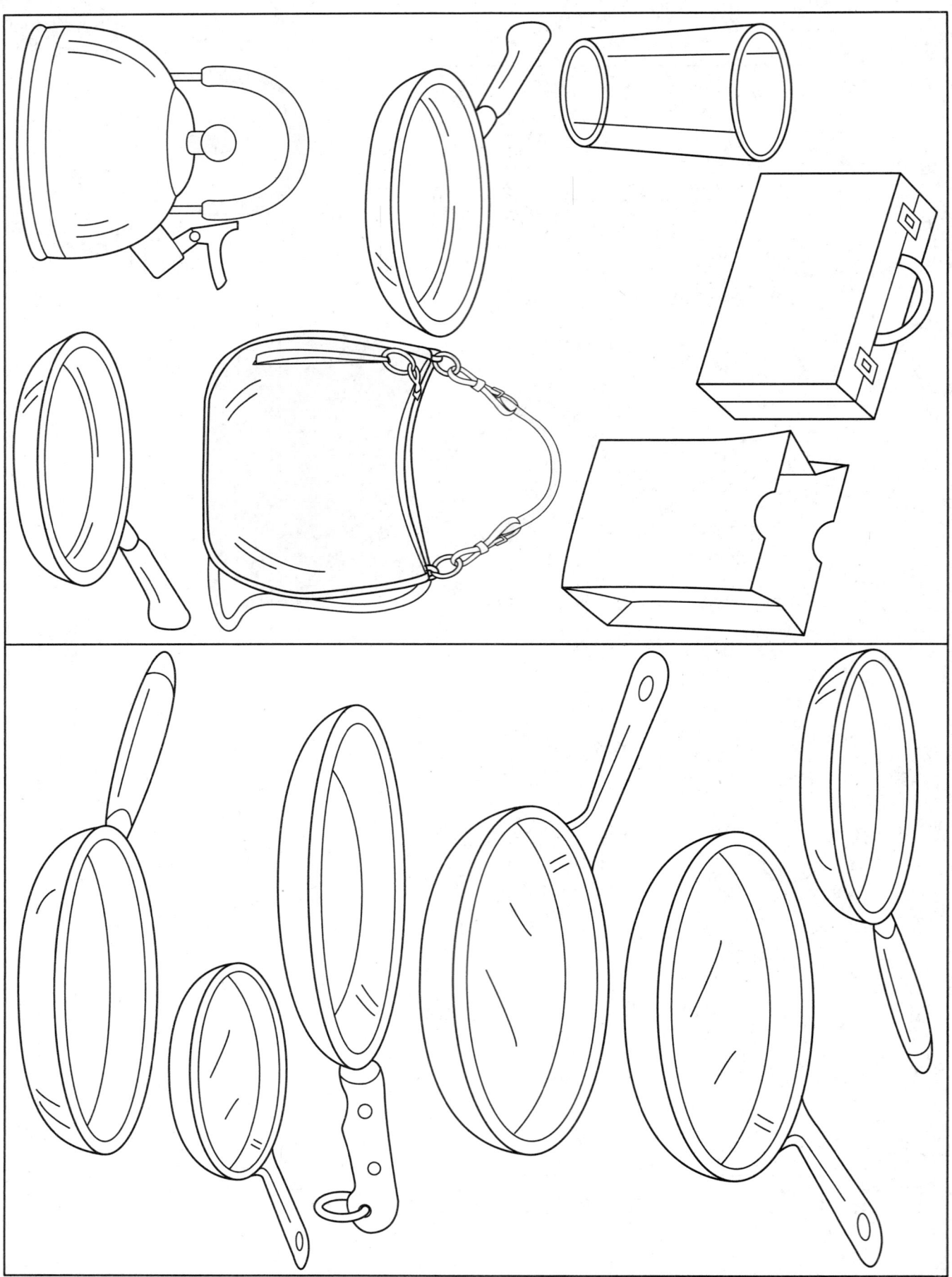

Side 2

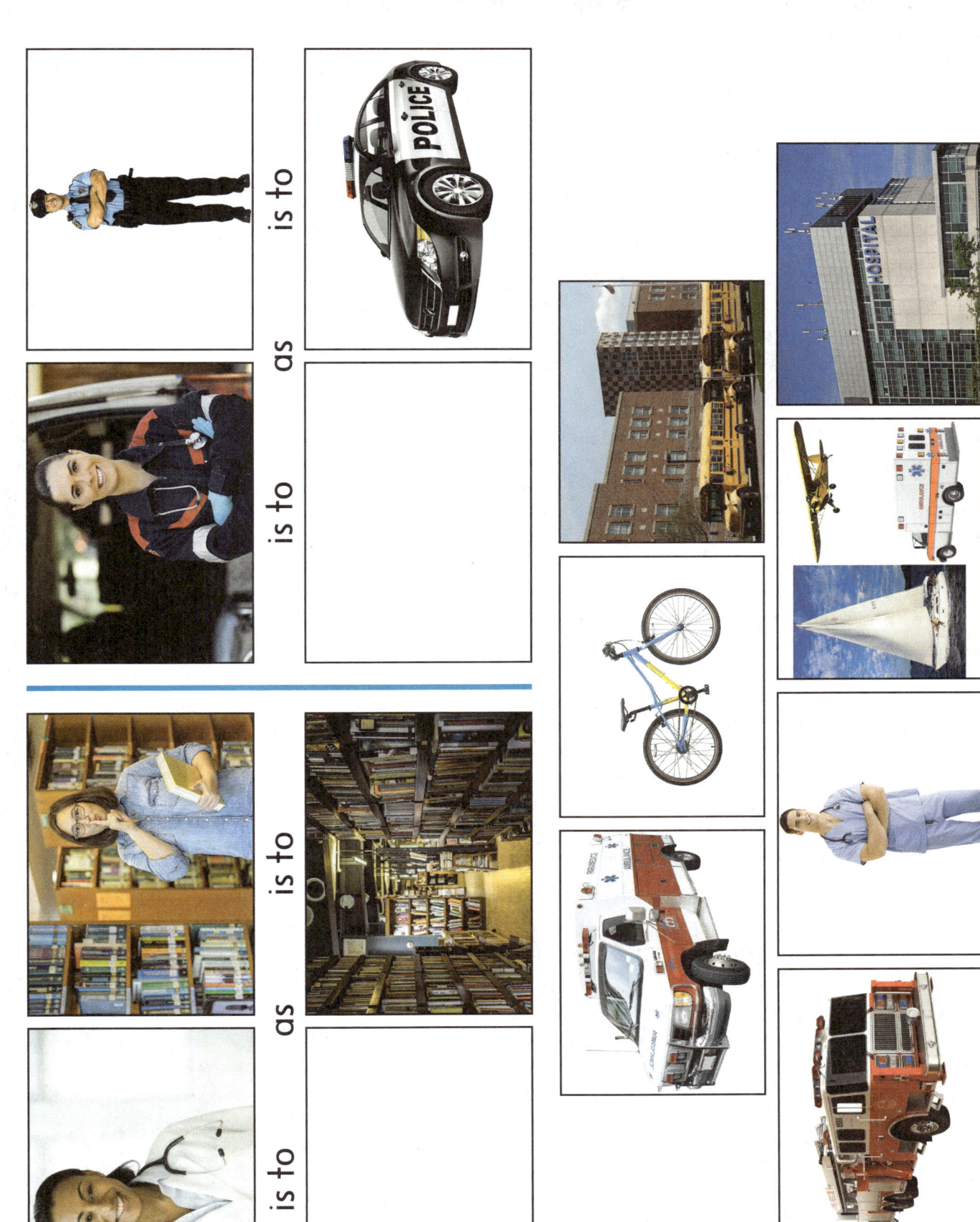

Side 3

Name

104

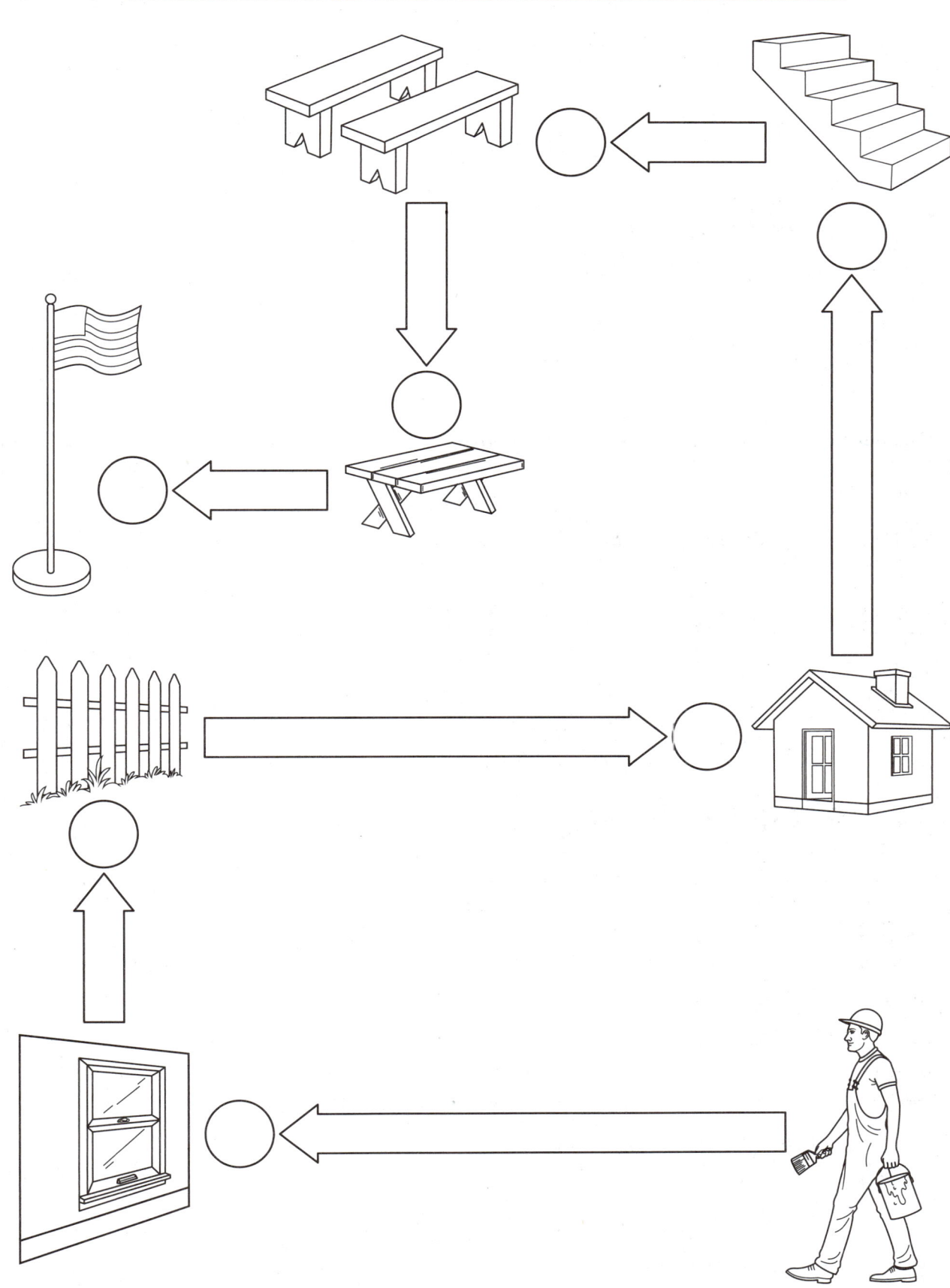

Side 1

True	False

1. Fish swim in water. _____

2. Eggs come from chickens. _____

3. Ice is hot. _____

---

under	easy	over	close to	above	hard

1. Put that bag below the bed.

2. Ice skating is difficult.

3. I live near a park.

Name _____ 105

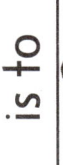 is to  as

 is to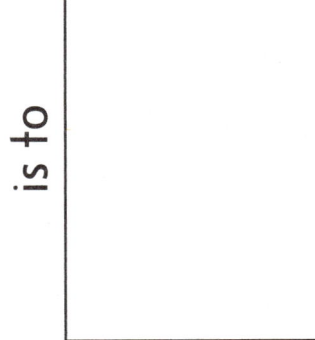

 is to 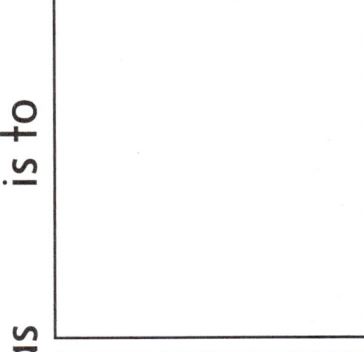 as

 is to

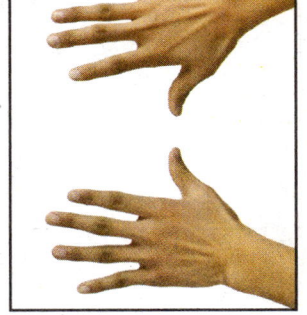

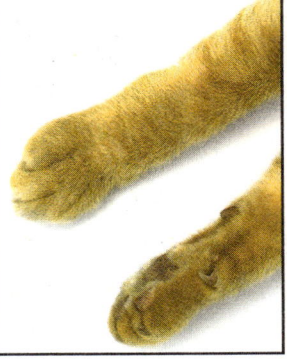

Side 1

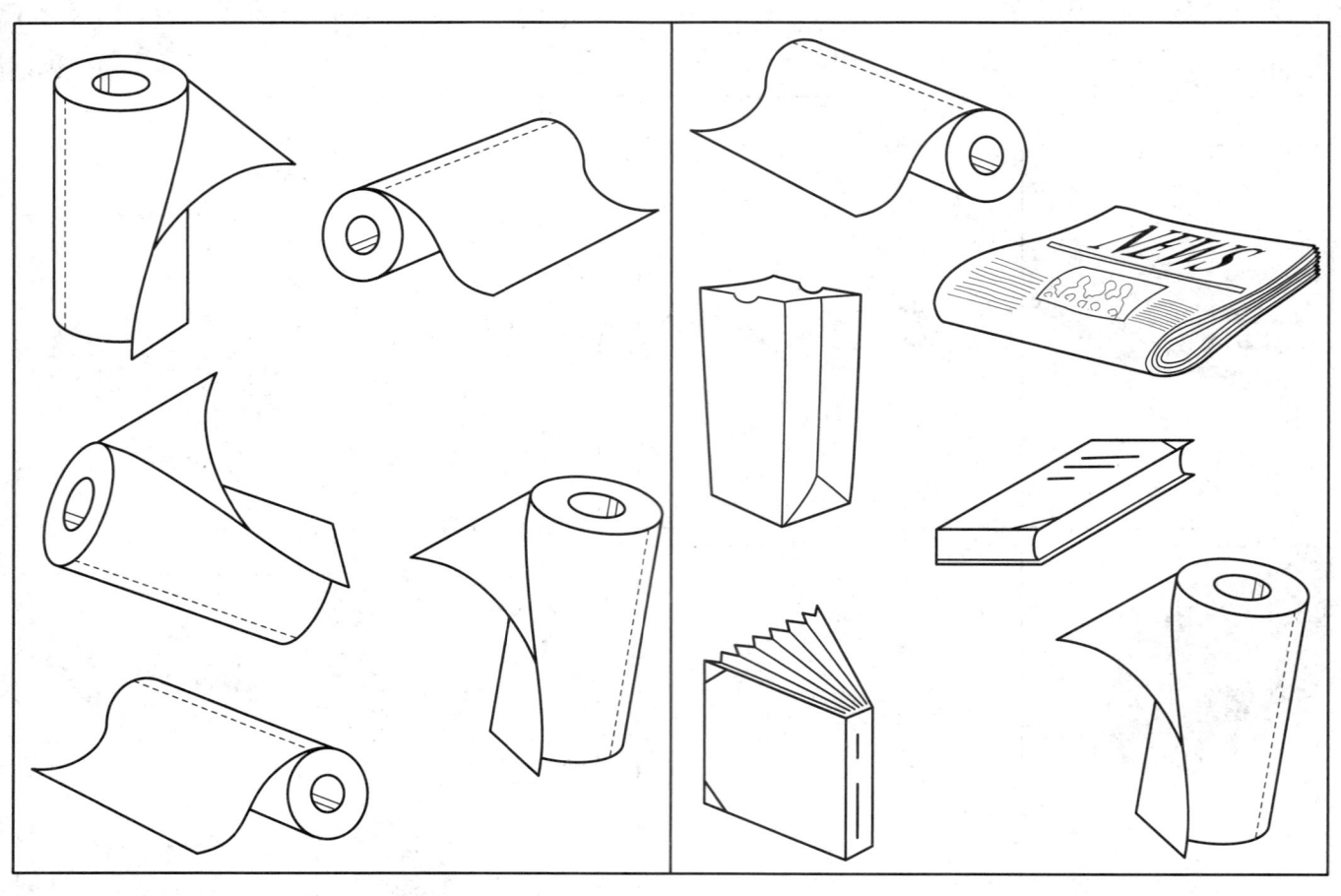

Today is _____.

1. i need paper pens and pencils

2. tuesday was cold and rainy

3. gordons party is on friday april 6

Name _____

106

 Hans Brinker, or The Silver Skates

 grasshopper

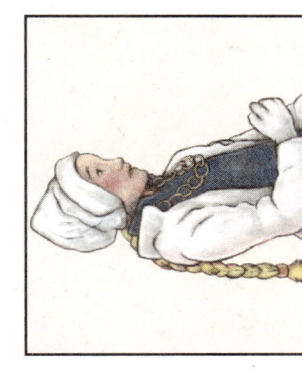 Gretel

 The Cat and the Bell

 ant

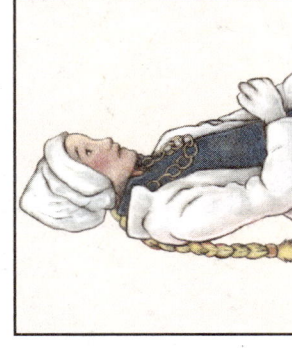 Hans

 The Ant and the Grasshopper

 shark

 wise old mouse

 Cindy the Squid

 Cindy

 Lester

Side 1

True   False

1. A window has a frame. _____

2. Cats have windows. _____

3. A window pane is made of glass. _____

4. A window can be dirty. _____

5. A window can be sick. _____

Name _____

| popcorn | reading | eating |

Side 1

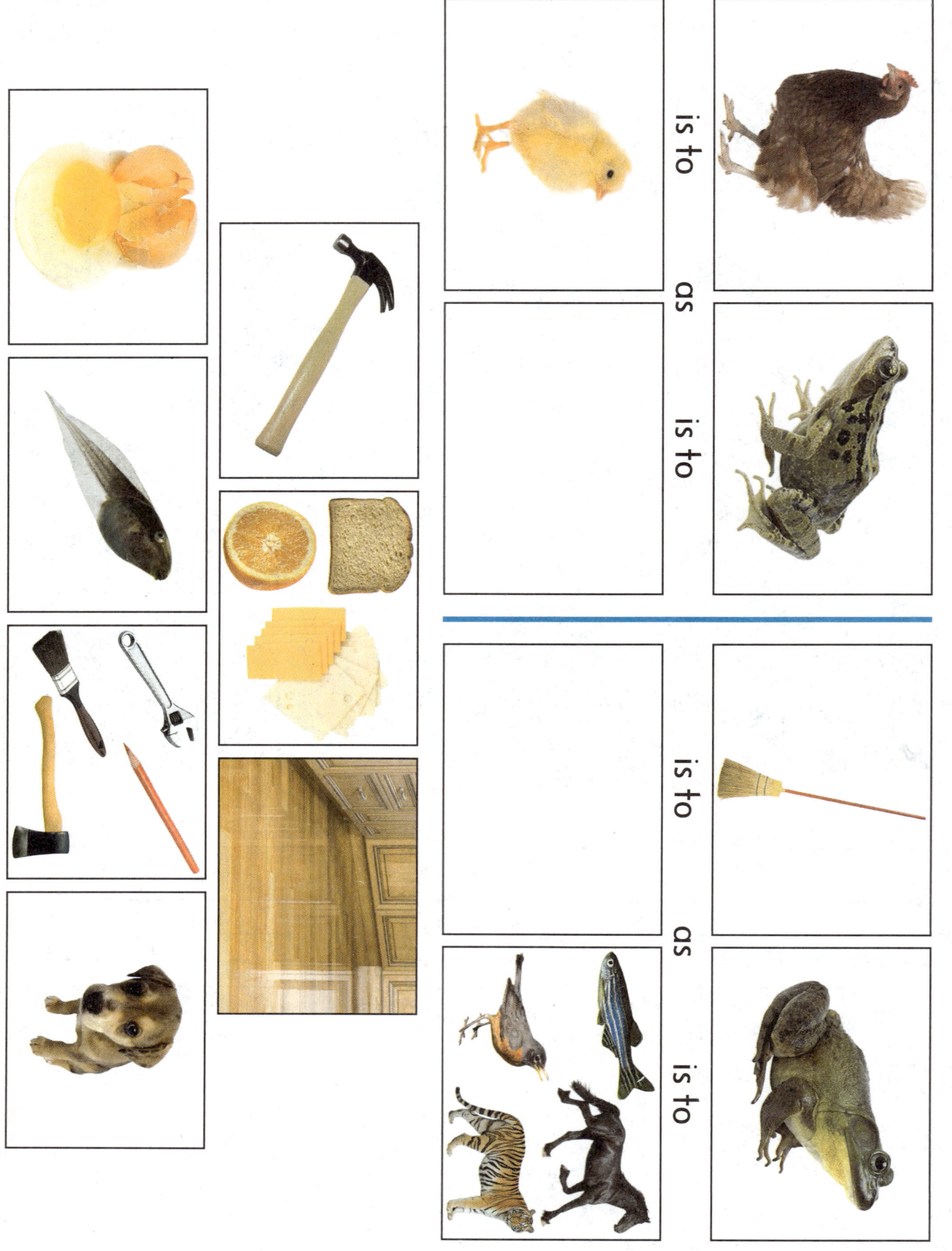

Name _____

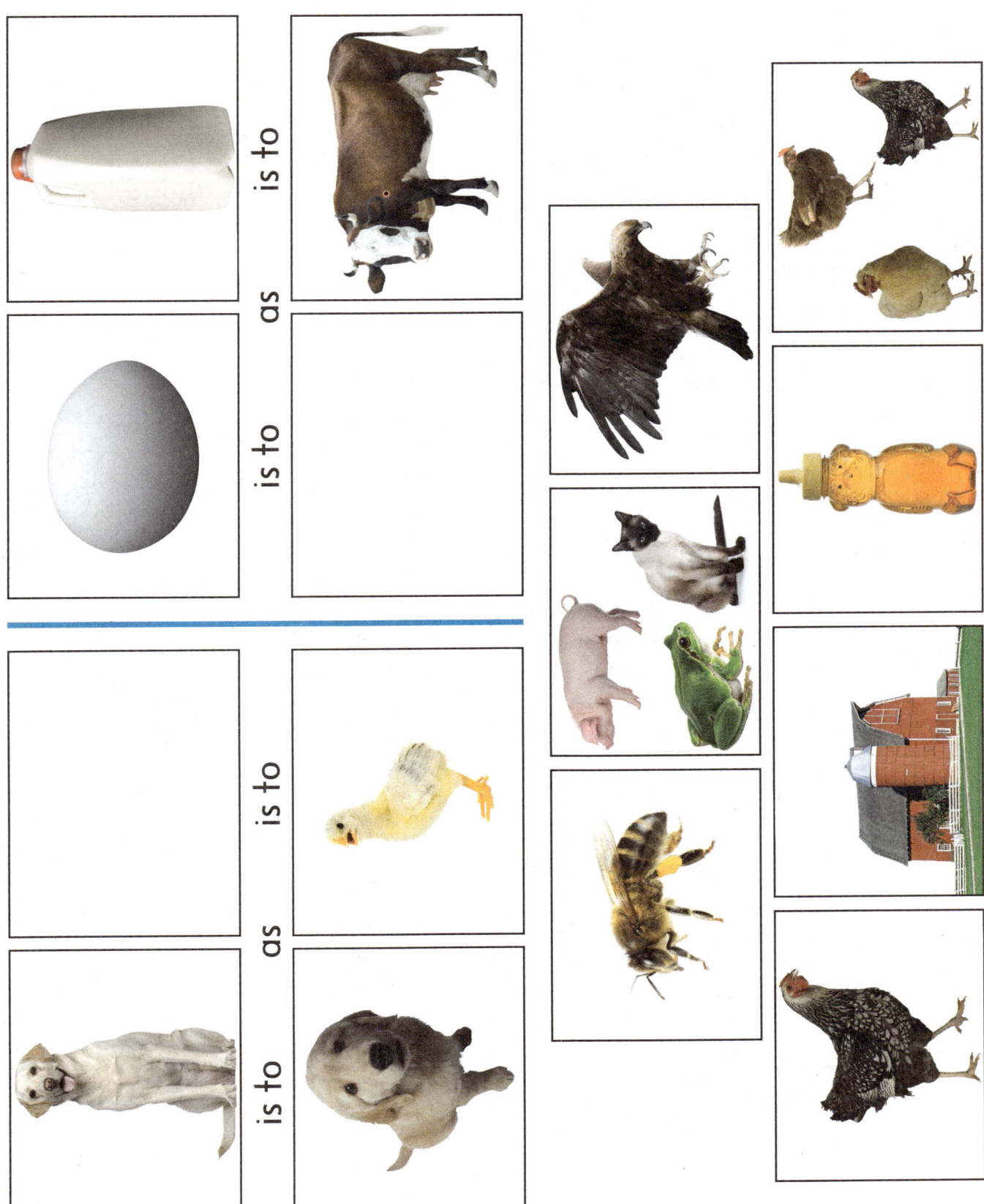

Side 2

Name _____

109

Side 1

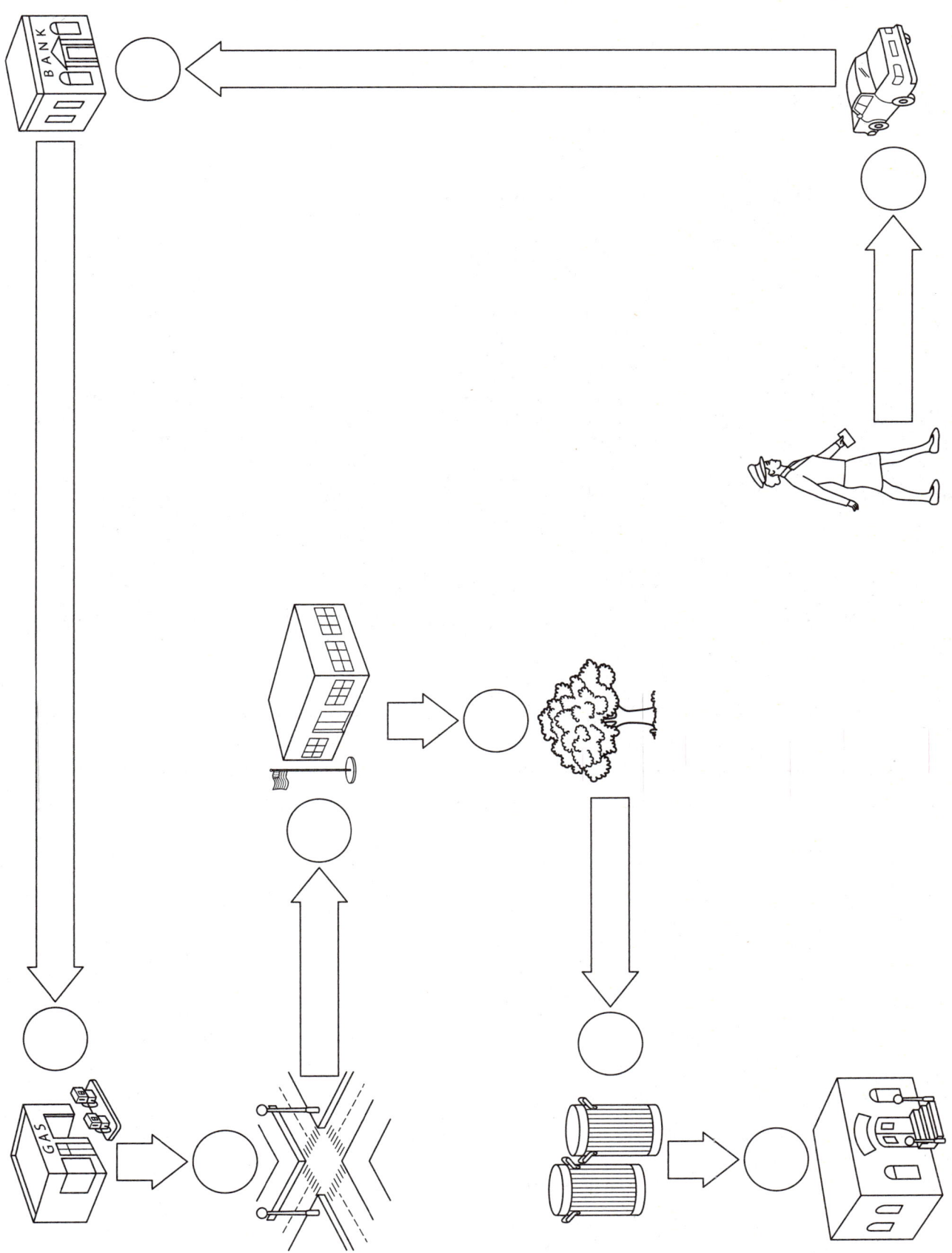

next	box	chair

Name _____

110

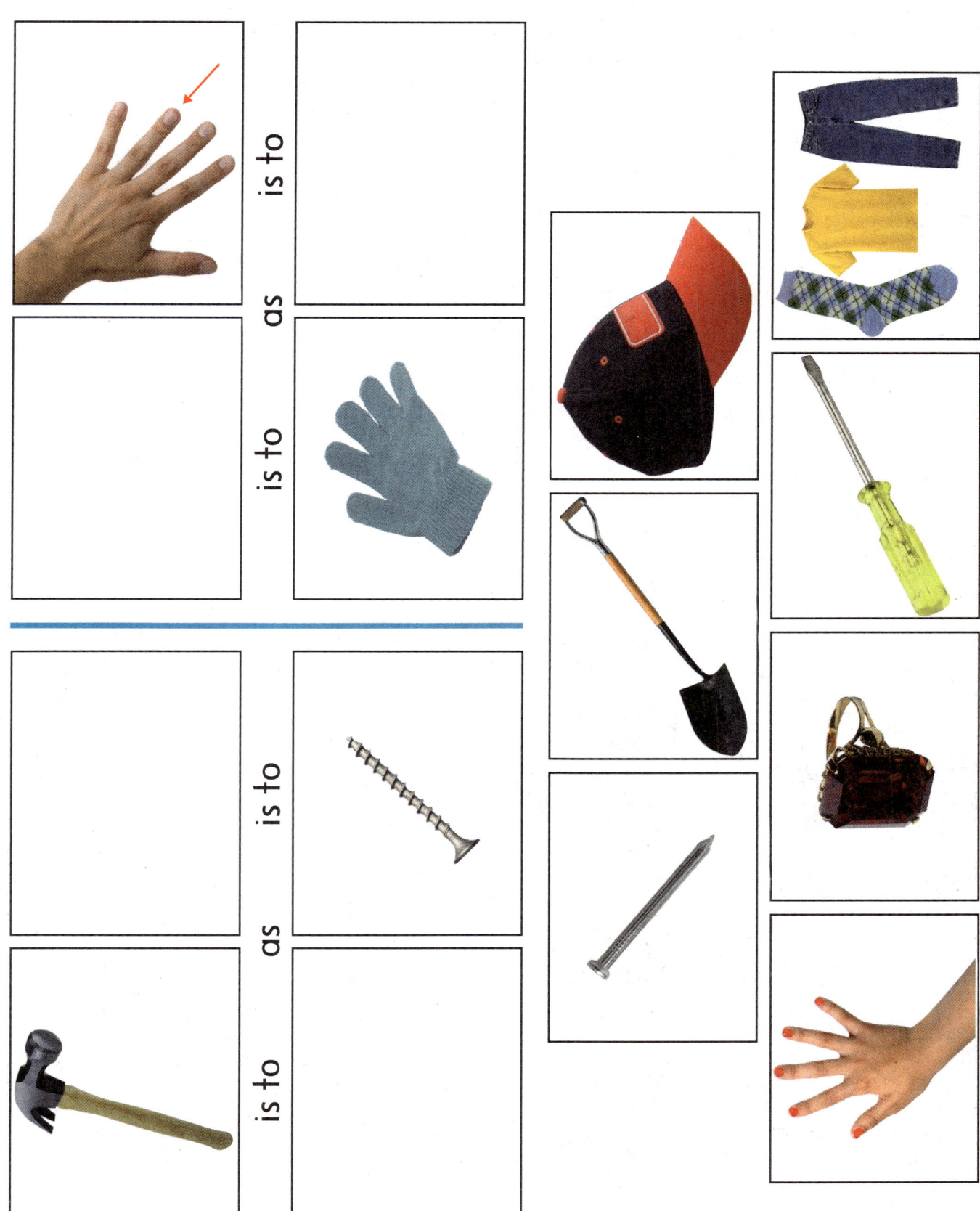

Side 1

Side 2

Name _____

111

Side 1

True   False

1. A cat is an animal. _ _ _ _

2. A cat is a plant. _ _ _ _

3. A cat is a living thing. _ _ _ _

4. A tree is an animal. _ _ _ _

5. A tree is a plant. _ _ _ _

6. A tree is a living thing. _ _ _ _

Name _____

112

the wise old mouse

Dr. Bookman

the ant

the wise old goat

Cindy

Ginger

1. Some characters are very smart.

2. I think _____ was the smartest character.

3. _____

4. _____

Side 1

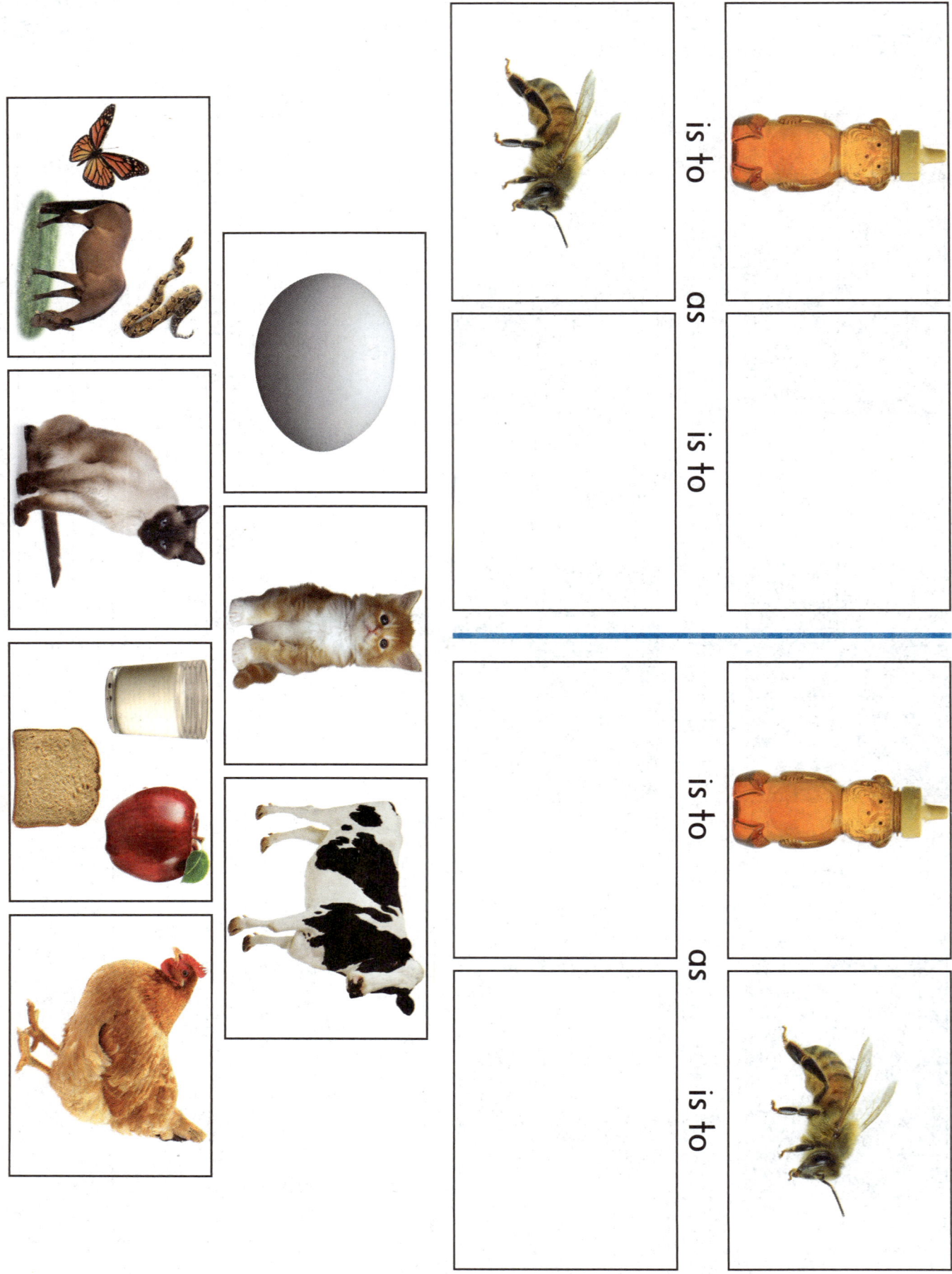

Name _____

| finish | large | start | easy | small |
| fat | difficult | after | soft |

1. I saw a **big** cat in the window.

S _____

O _____

2. That game is **hard** to play.

S _____

O _____

3. Will the rain **end** soon?

S _____

O _____

Side 1

	containers	furniture	buildings

glass _____   school _____

chair _____   bed _____

hospital _____   suitcase _____

couch _____   house _____

box _____   wallet _____

Name

114

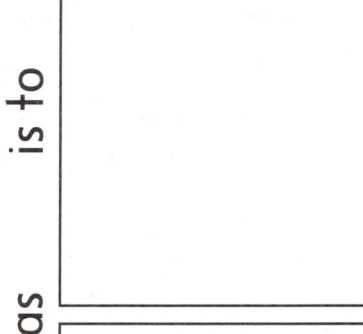 is to 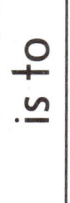 as

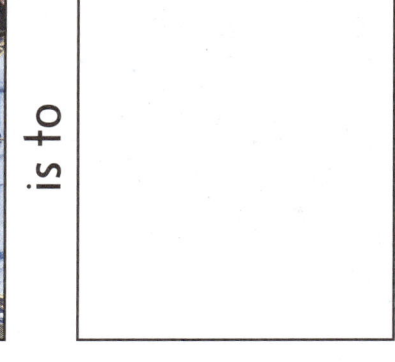 is to

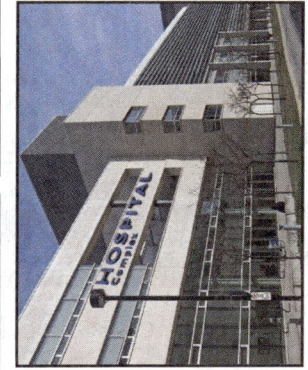

 is to  as

 is to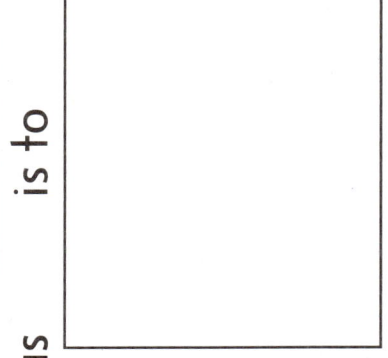

Side 1

| jumped | catch | played | rope |

Name _____

near   below   sick   skinny   loud
over   empty   quiet   well

1. The bird flew **under** a cloud.

S _____

O _____

2. Is it **noisy** in the park?

S _____

O _____

3. Your sister looks **healthy** today.

S _____

O _____

Side 1

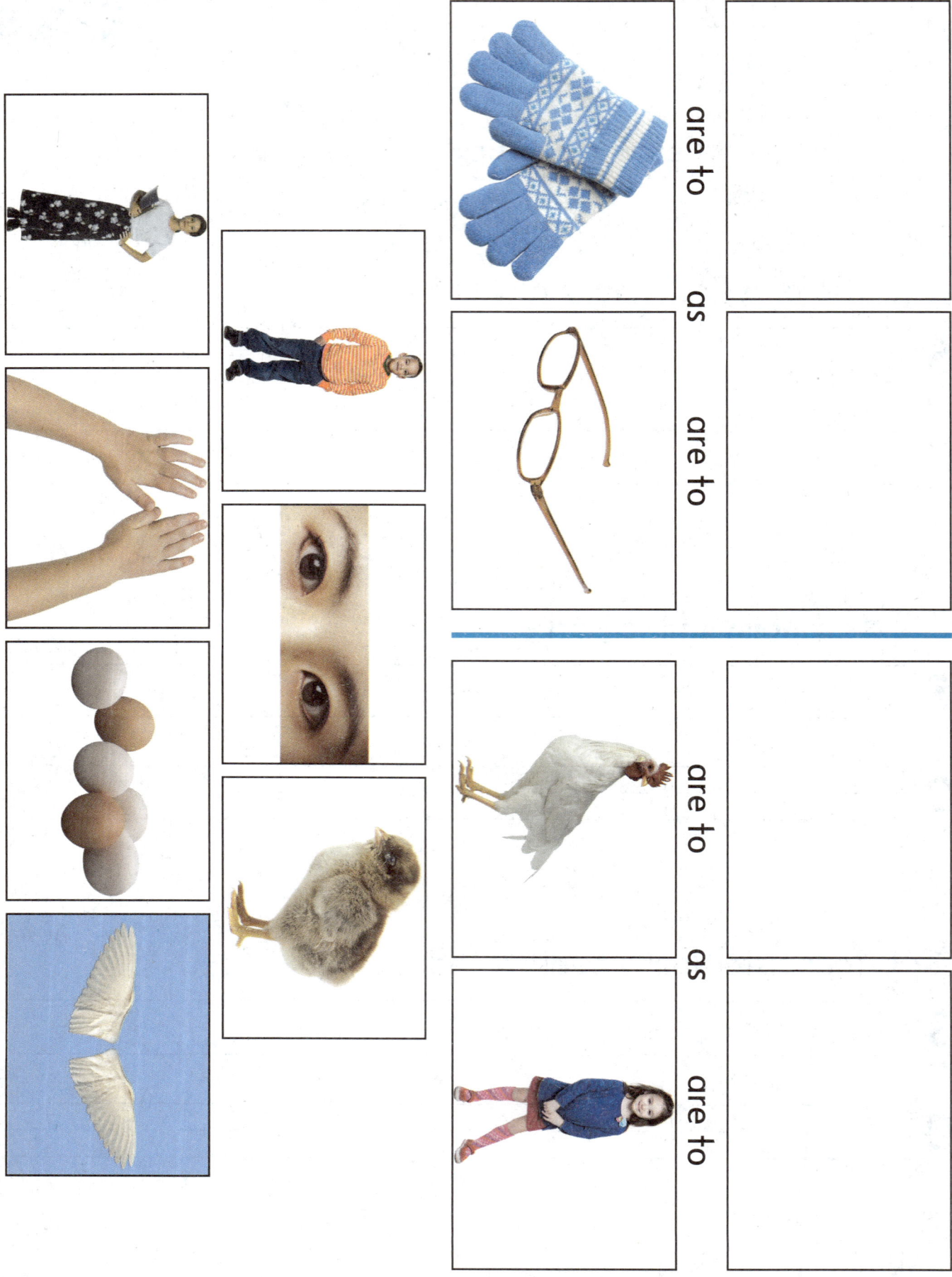

Side 2

Name _____ 116

Frogs on a Log   A Circus and A Smile   Hole in a Bucket

| winter | spring | summer | fall |

_____
_____
_____
_____
_____
_____

Side 1

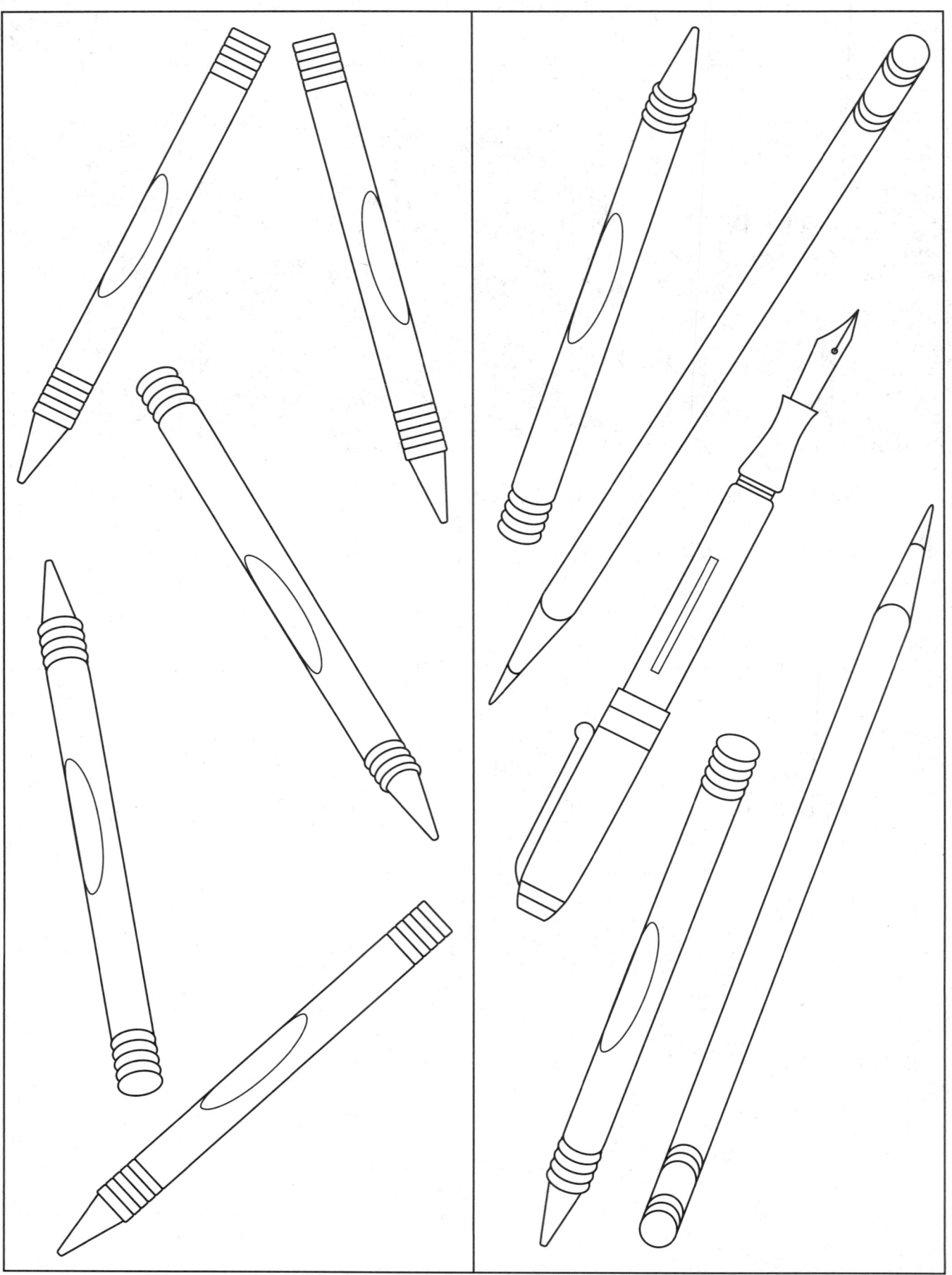

Side 2

Name _____ 117

Side 1

sawed   painted   woman   board

Side 2

Name _____

| 118 |

shut　　　fat　　　open　　　near　　　weeping
skinny　　empty　　laughing　　happy

1. I will **close** the door.

S _____

O _____

2. Is she **crying**?

S _____

O _____

3. My cat is too **thin**.

S _____

O _____

Side 1

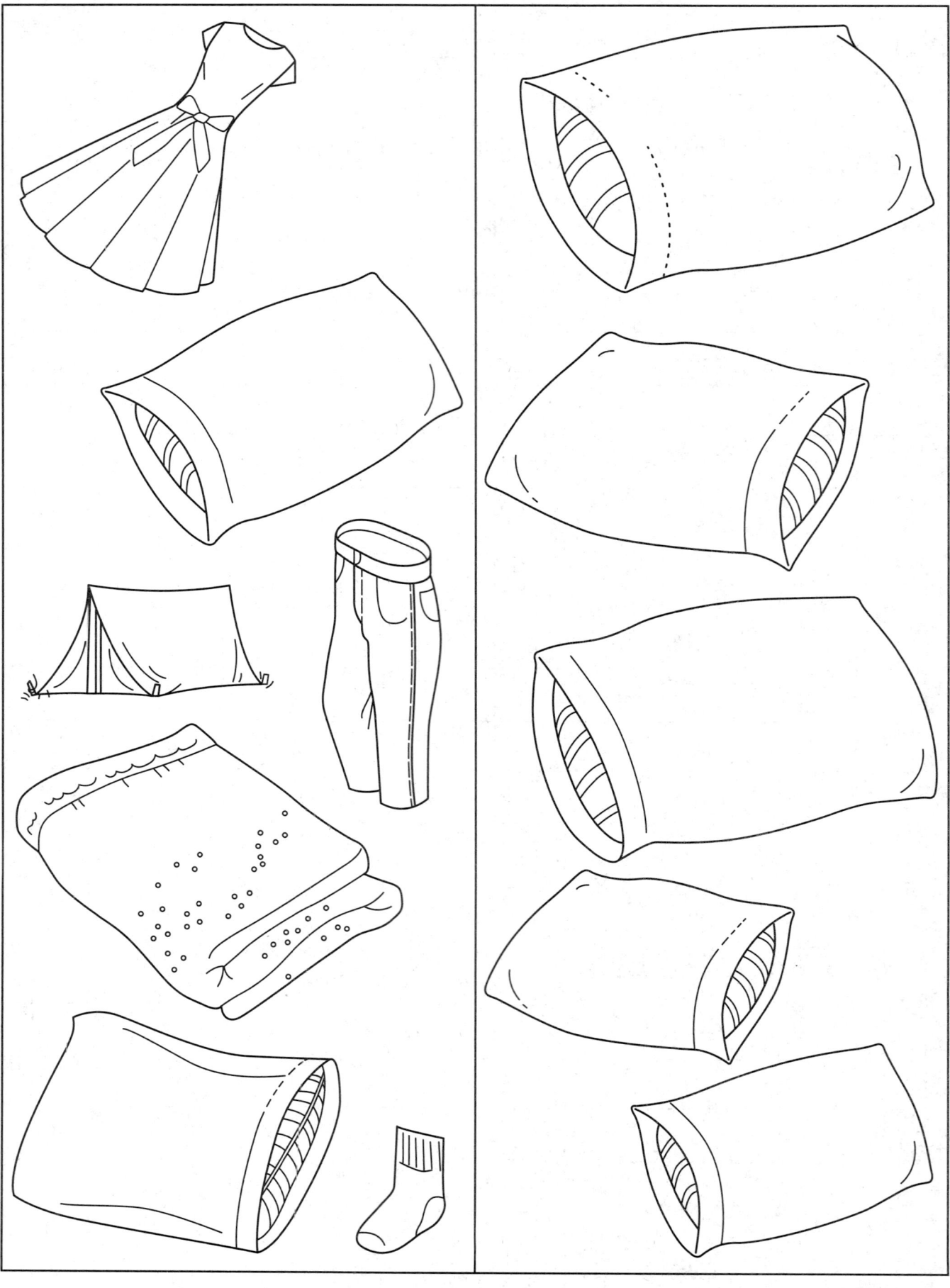

Side 2

Name

119

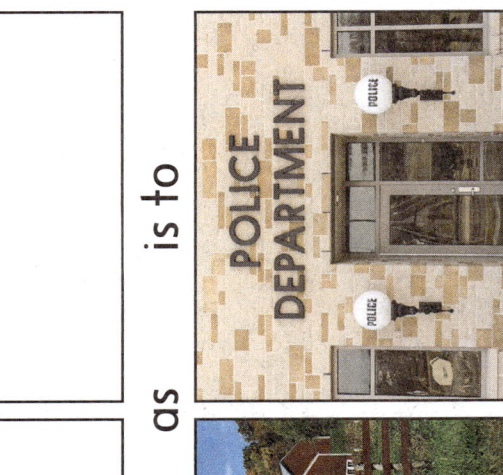

☐ is to as ☐ is to

☐ is to as ☐ is to

Side 1

dog   table   sitting   window
sad   afraid   feels   floor

Side 2

Name _____

120

Side 1

elephant	tree	shade	feels
very	little	under

Name _____

| deciduous | bark | palm | canopy |
| evergreen | temperate | conifer | tropical |

1. A _____ tree has cones and needles.

2. A _____ climate stays hot and wet all year.

3. An _____ tree does not lose all its leaves every year.

4. A _____ climate changes from hot in the summer to cold in the winter.

5. A _____ is a thick layer of leaves from many trees.

6. A _____ tree loses all its leaves every year.

girl   jealous   happy   cat
kneeling   mad   patting   dog

Side 2

Name _____

True   False

1. An evergreen tree loses all its leaves in the winter. _____
2. Leaves make sugar from sunlight and water. _____
3. Leaves add oxygen to the air. _____
4. Leaves add carbon dioxide to the air. _____
5. Bark collects water for the tree. _____
6. A canopy makes air cooler in a forest. _____
7. Trees are the tallest kind of plant. _____
8. A deciduous tree has green leaves in the winter. _____

boy   running   from   afraid
chasing   squirrel   excited

Side 2

Name _____

123

___ is to ___ as nails are to hammer

___ is to ___ as screwdriver is to screws

Side 1

Side 2

brown   hungry   monkey   wants   eating
share   black   will   banana

Name

124

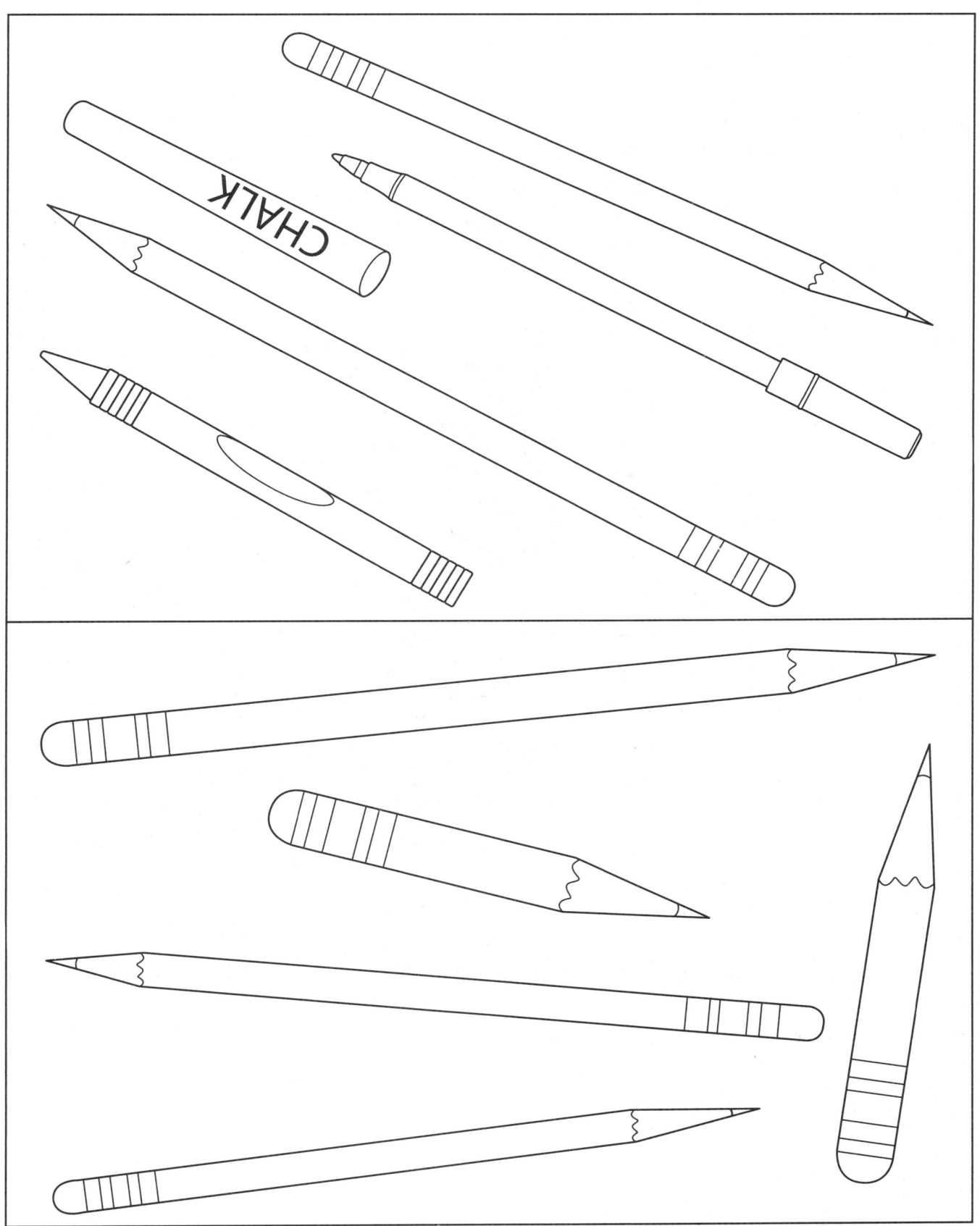

Side 1

boat sitting happy smiling feels fishing

Side 2

Name _____

125

Side 1

waving   hiding   floor   angry
sitting   chair   broke   scared

Side 2

Name _____

126

| canopy adaptations woodpeckers hibernate |
| recreation sloths logging temperate |

1. _____ have sharp beaks to peck through tree bark.

2. Camping and hiking are types of _____.

3. Black bears _____ all winter long.

4. _____ help plants and animals to live in their environment.

5. _____ provides humans with wood from forests.

6. _____ cling to branches with long, powerful claws.

Side 1

fish   lake   swimming   dog   chasing   water

Side 2

Name _____

True False

1. An adaptation helps an animal to survive. ___ ___

2. Black bears live in tropical climates. ___ ___

3. Woodpeckers live in temperate climates. ___ ___

4. A canopy makes air warmer in a forest. ___ ___

5. A canopy makes shade for plants and animals. ___ ___

6. Logging provides humans with metal. ___ ___

7. Hiking and camping are types of recreation. ___ ___

8. Sloths hibernate during the winter. ___ ___

playing   monkey   sitting   truck   piano   man

Side 2

Name _____

128

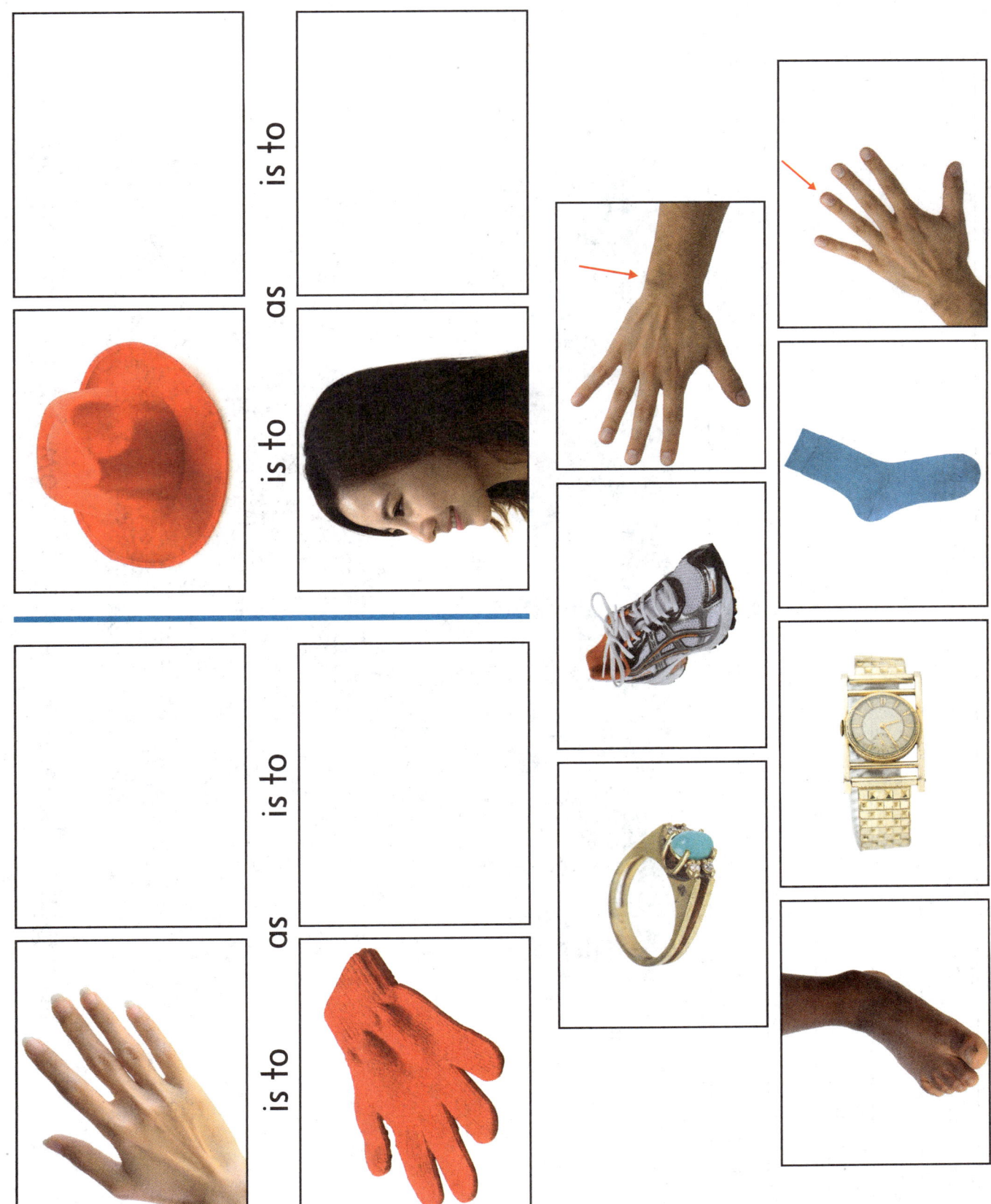

Side 1

doghouse bird water bone chewing drinking

Side 2

Name _____

129

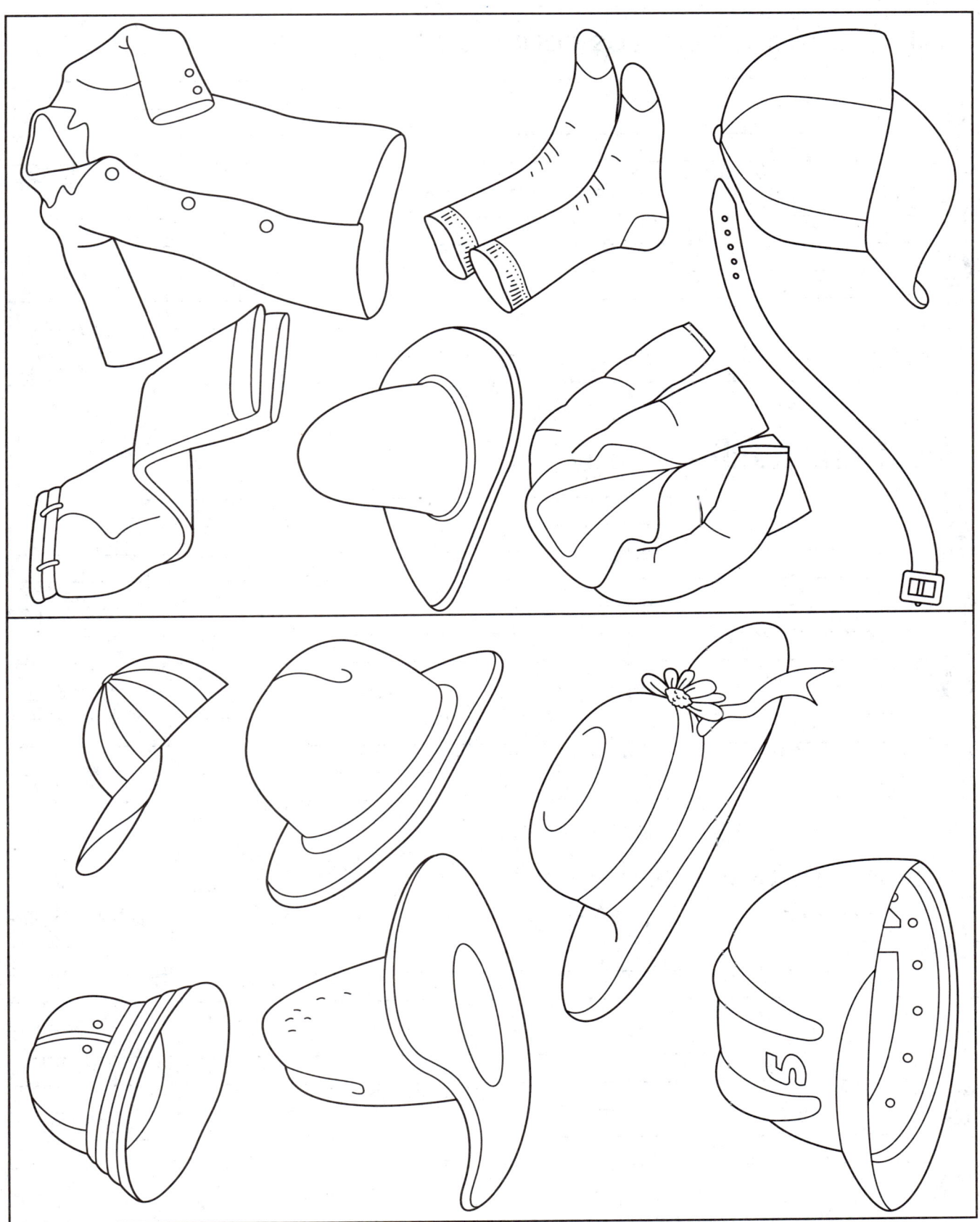

Side 1

soft   quiet   easy   well   narrow   difficult   sick   loud

1. The math test was very **hard**.

S _____

O _____

2. I feel **healthy** today.

S _____

O _____

3. It was **noisy** at the park.

S _____

O _____

Name _____

130

plants	food	materials

cheese _____ metal _____

fern _____ vine _____

cloth _____ honey _____

soup _____ concrete _____

grass _____ flower _____

Side 1

girl hair ground combing cat swing sleeping

Side 2

Name

131

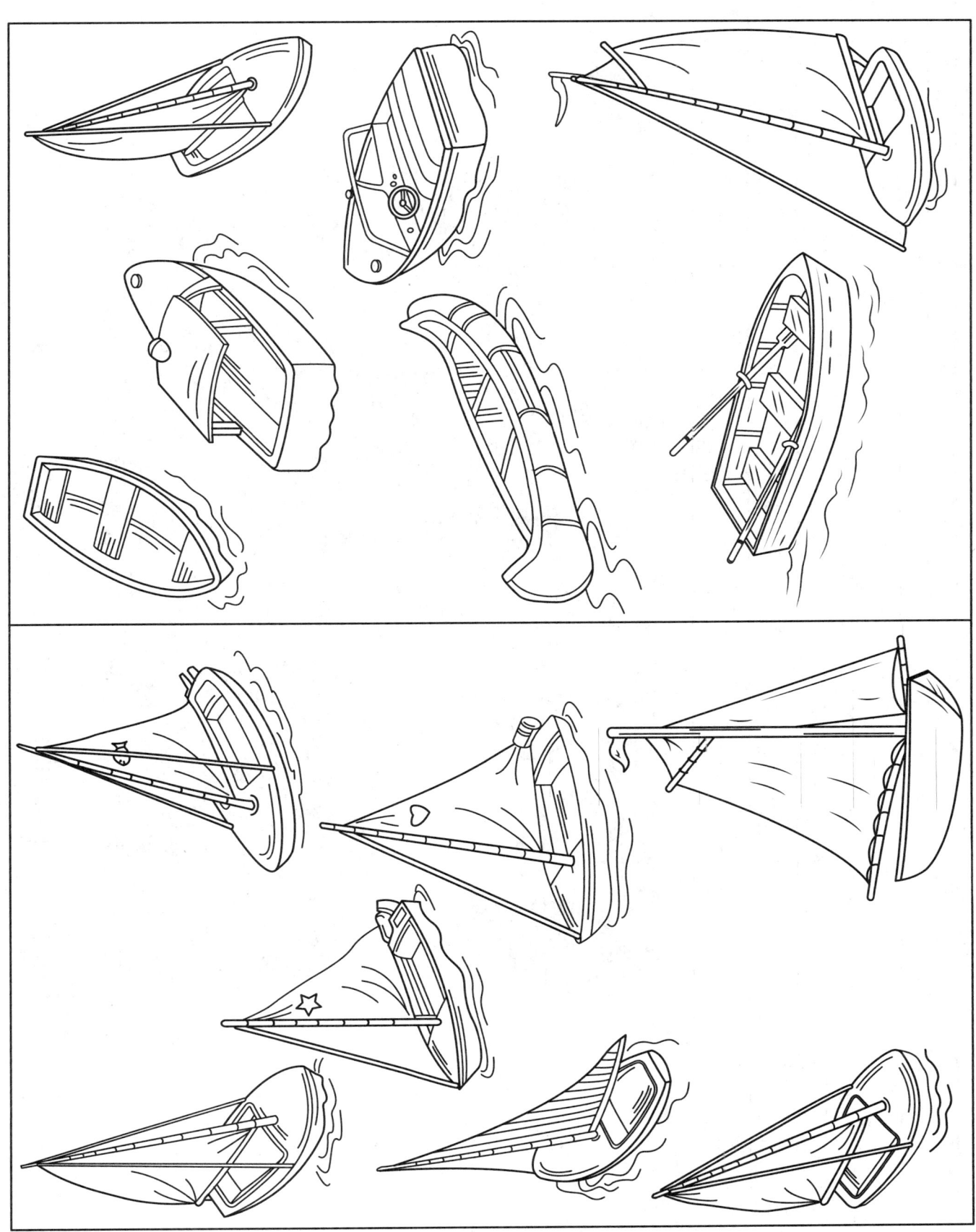

Side 1

porch   tree   nut   eating   squirrel   climb

Side 2

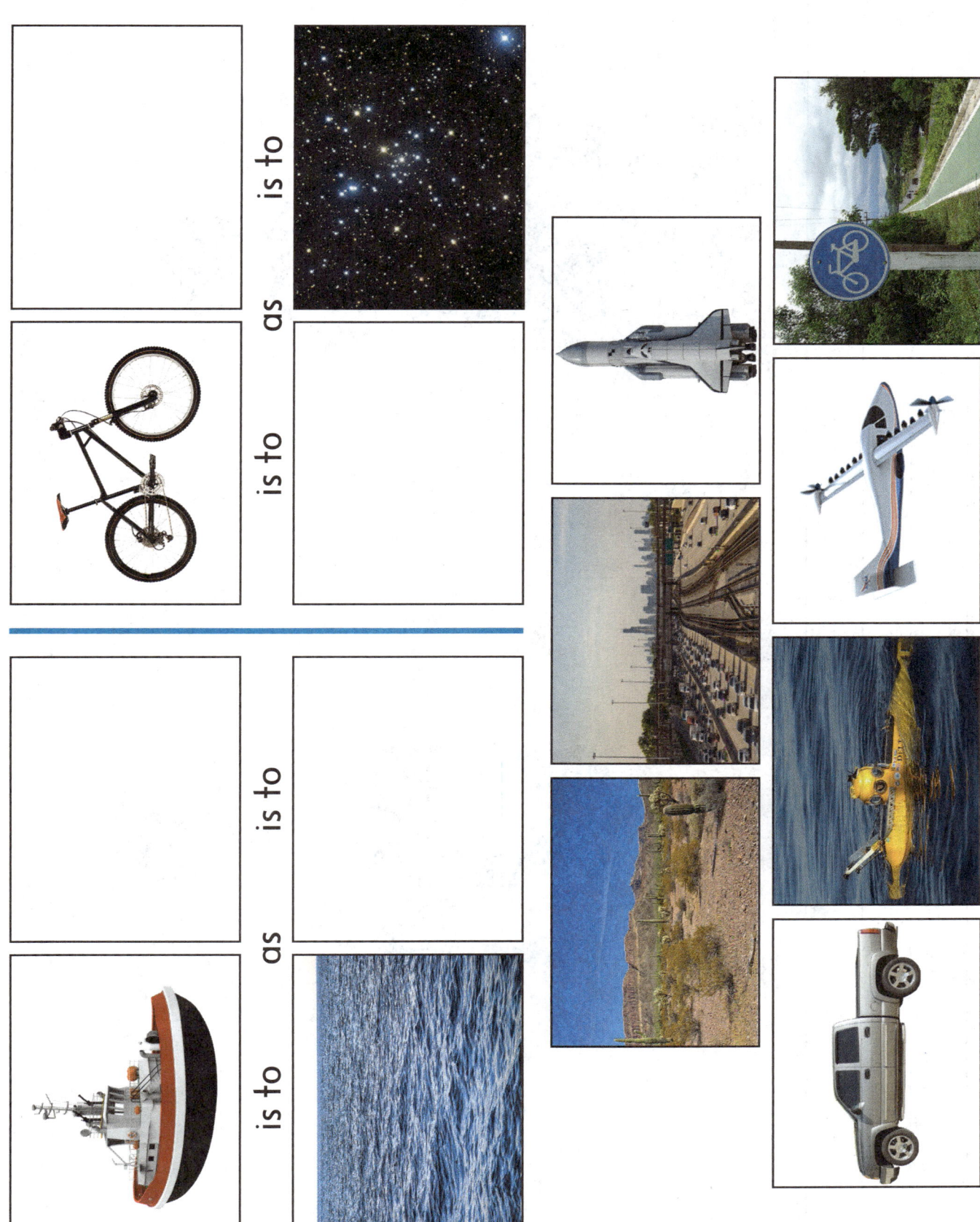

chair　woman　sitting　painting

Side 2

Name _____

133

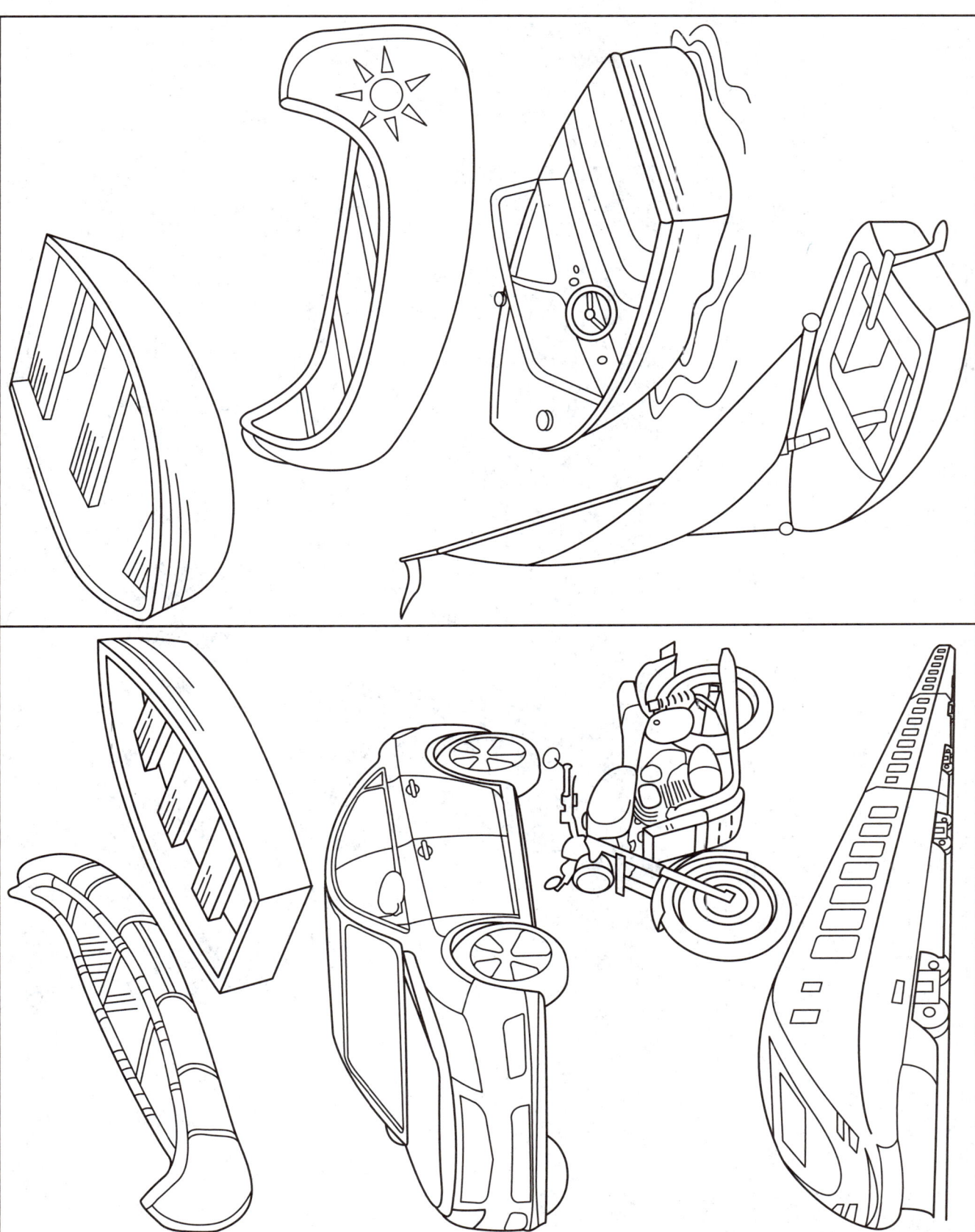

Side 1

over excited cake kitchen woman happy

Side 2

Name _____

134

 is to  as 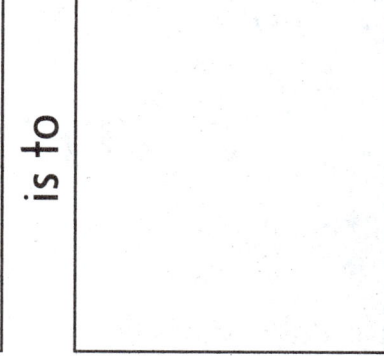 is to _____

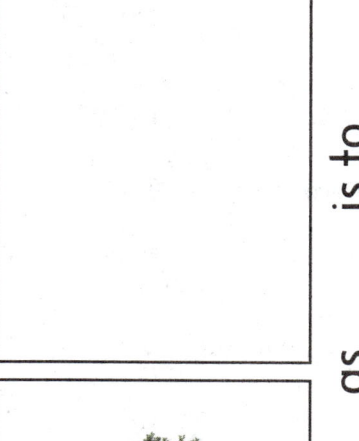 is to 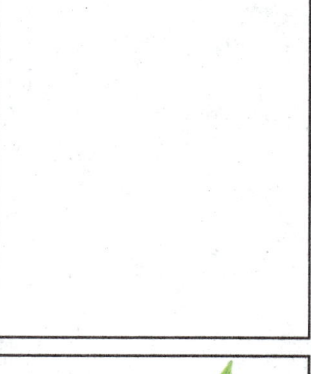 as _____ is to _____

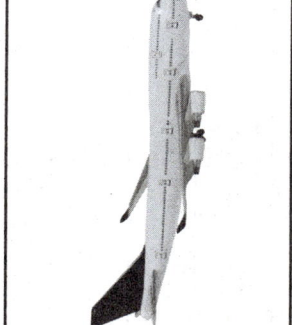
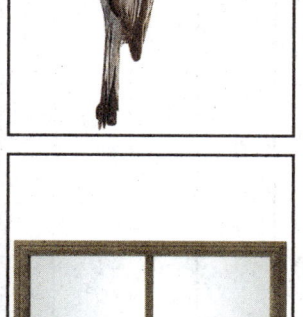

Side 1

Side 2

Name _____

135

Side 1

Side 2

car   eating   reading   book   brother   apple

Name _____

| savanna | shrub | wildflower | steppe |
| scarcity | prairie | latex | |

1. _____ is a poisonous liquid in the trunk and branches of trees.

2. A _____ is the main type of tropical grassland.

3. A _____ is a temperate grassland with tall grasses and some larger plants.

4. A _____ of water prevents larger plants from growing.

5. A _____ is a temperate grassland with short grasses and almost no larger plants.

6. A _____ is a woody plant smaller than a tree.

turtle scared confused
are standing howling

Side 2

Name _____

True   False

1. A scarcity of water stops larger plants from growing. ____ ____

2. Animals that eat latex may get sick or die. ____ ____

3. Shrubs are woody plants that grow taller than most trees. ____ ____

4. A savanna gets heavy rain in the summer. ____ ____

5. There is a scarcity of shade under a canopy of trees. ____ ____

6. Some grasses are taller than people. ____ ____

7. A steppe gets colder winters than a savanna. ____ ____

8. A steppe gets more rain than a prairie. ____ ____

Side 1

Side 2

Name

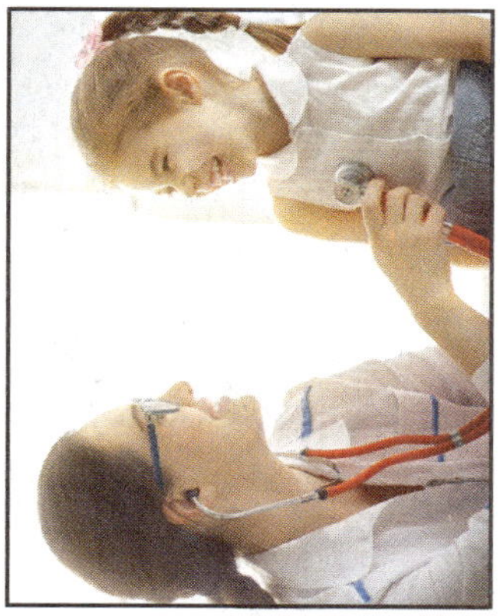

is to

as

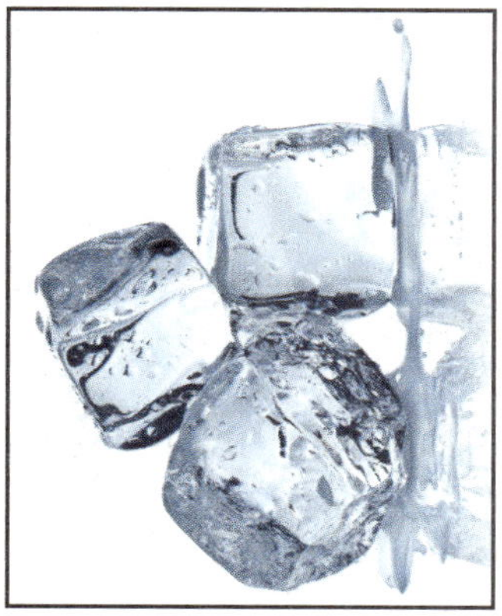

is to

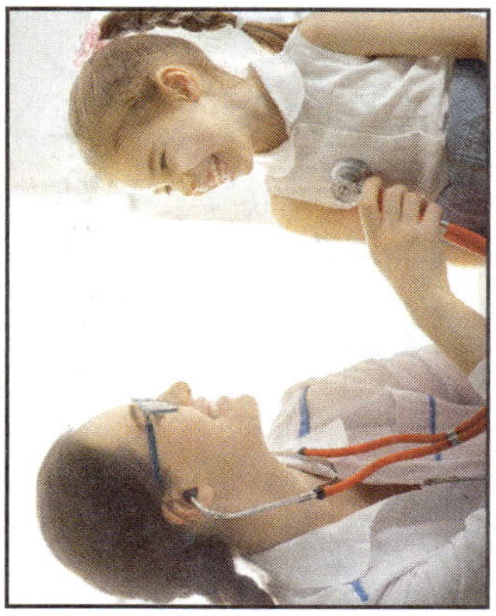

is to

as

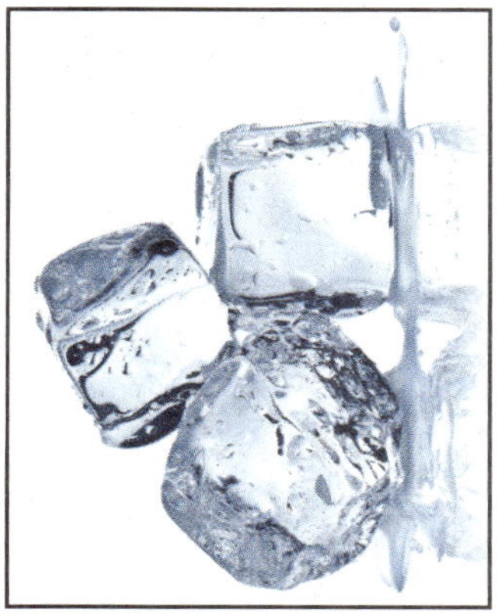

is to

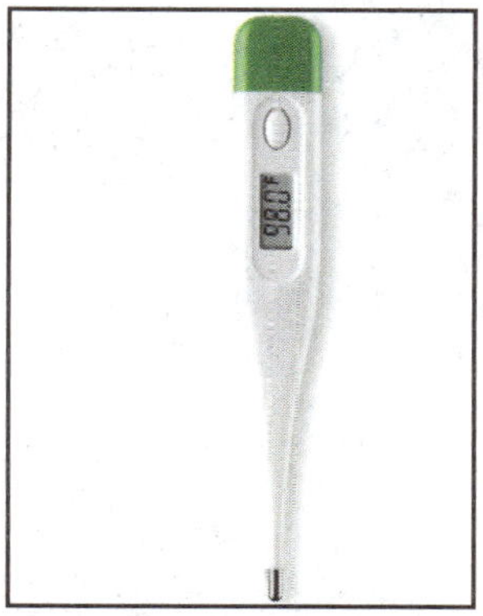

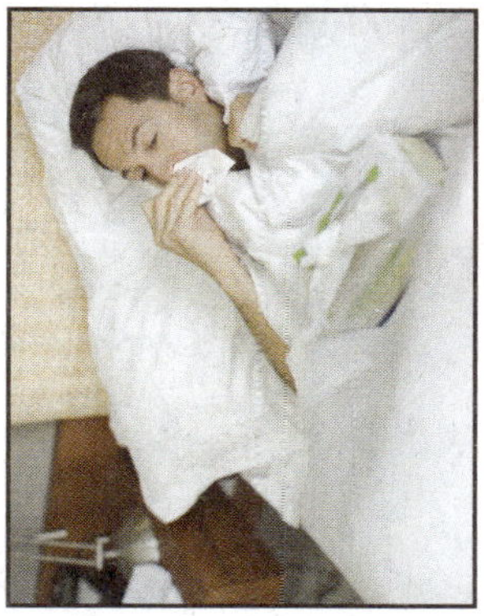

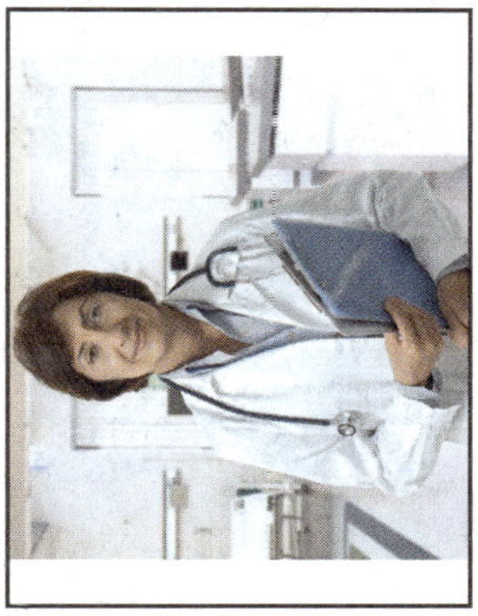

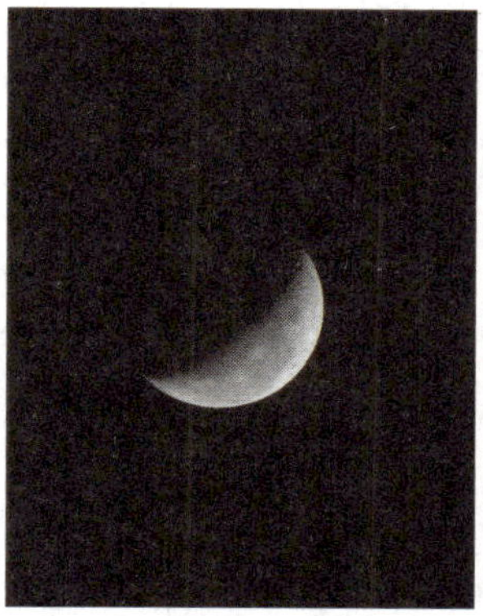

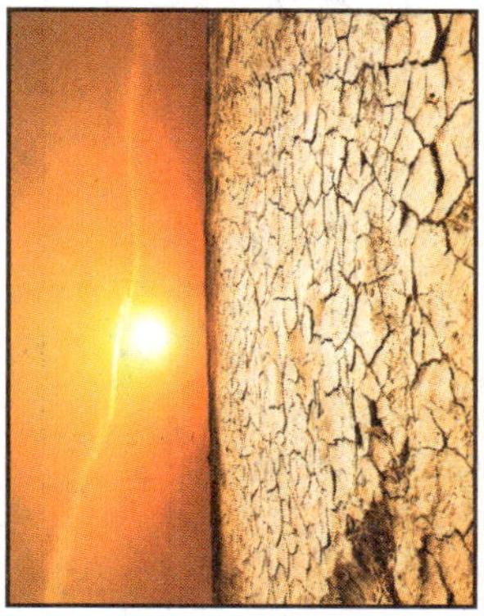

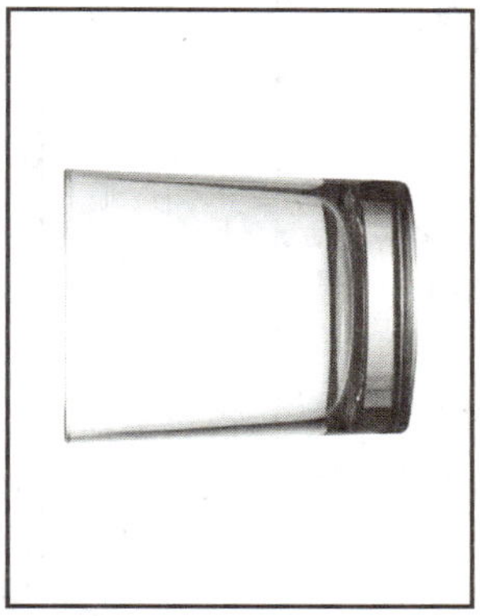

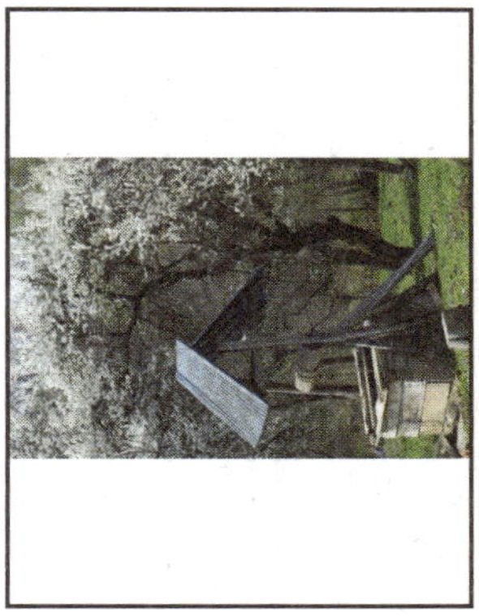

mopped   washed   dishes   floor

Side 2

Name _____

139

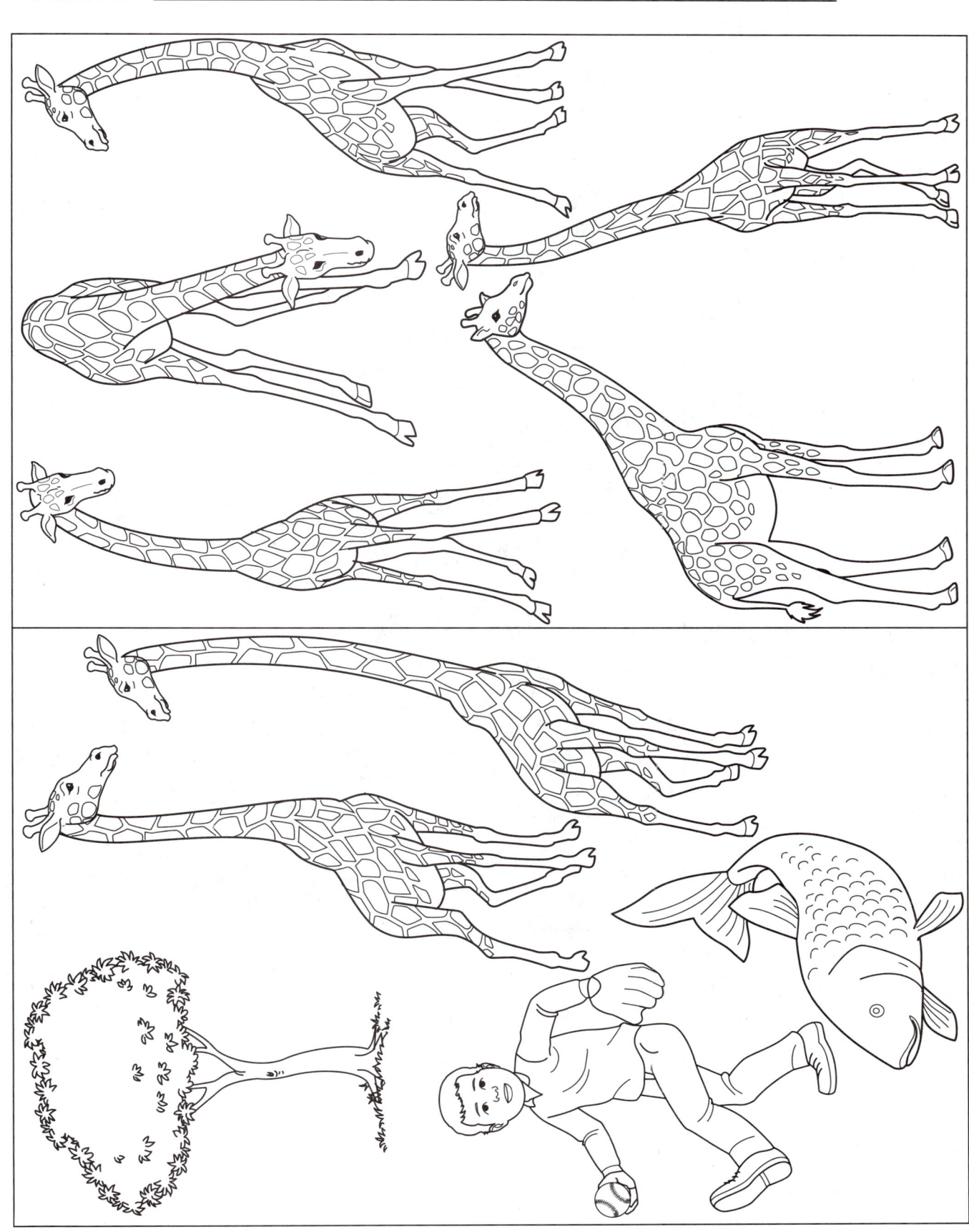

Side 1

sled   sitting   pulling   horses

Side 2

Name _____

140

Side 1

weak   weep   dirty   throw   laugh   late   pull   sick

1. That dog is very strong.

2. The car was clean yesterday.

3. I am reading a book that makes me cry.

4. Can we go to the store early on Saturday?

5. Josh will push the sled through the snow.

Name _____

| cattle | rabbits | herbivores | humans |
| woodpeckers | giraffes | bison | |

1. _____ migrate across large areas to find grass.

2. _____ dig burrows in the soil to hide and stay warm.

3. _____ graze on open grasslands.

4. _____ irrigate fields to grow crops.

5. _____ make nests in poisonous trees.

6. _____ eat leaves from the tops of acacia trees.

sleeping   lions   zoo   looking

Name _____

| True | False |

1. Acacia trees can form small, thin canopies on a savanna. ____

2. Both animals and plants have adaptations that help them to survive. ____

3. All herbivores migrate to find food. ____

4. Rabbits dig burrows that form a warren underground. ____

5. Bison have very poor eyesight. ____

6. Farmers graze animals on open grasslands to save money. ____

7. Rabbits can run much faster than bison. ____

8. Woodpeckers only live in temperate climates. ____

Side 1

ate spotted corn white goat grass

Name

144

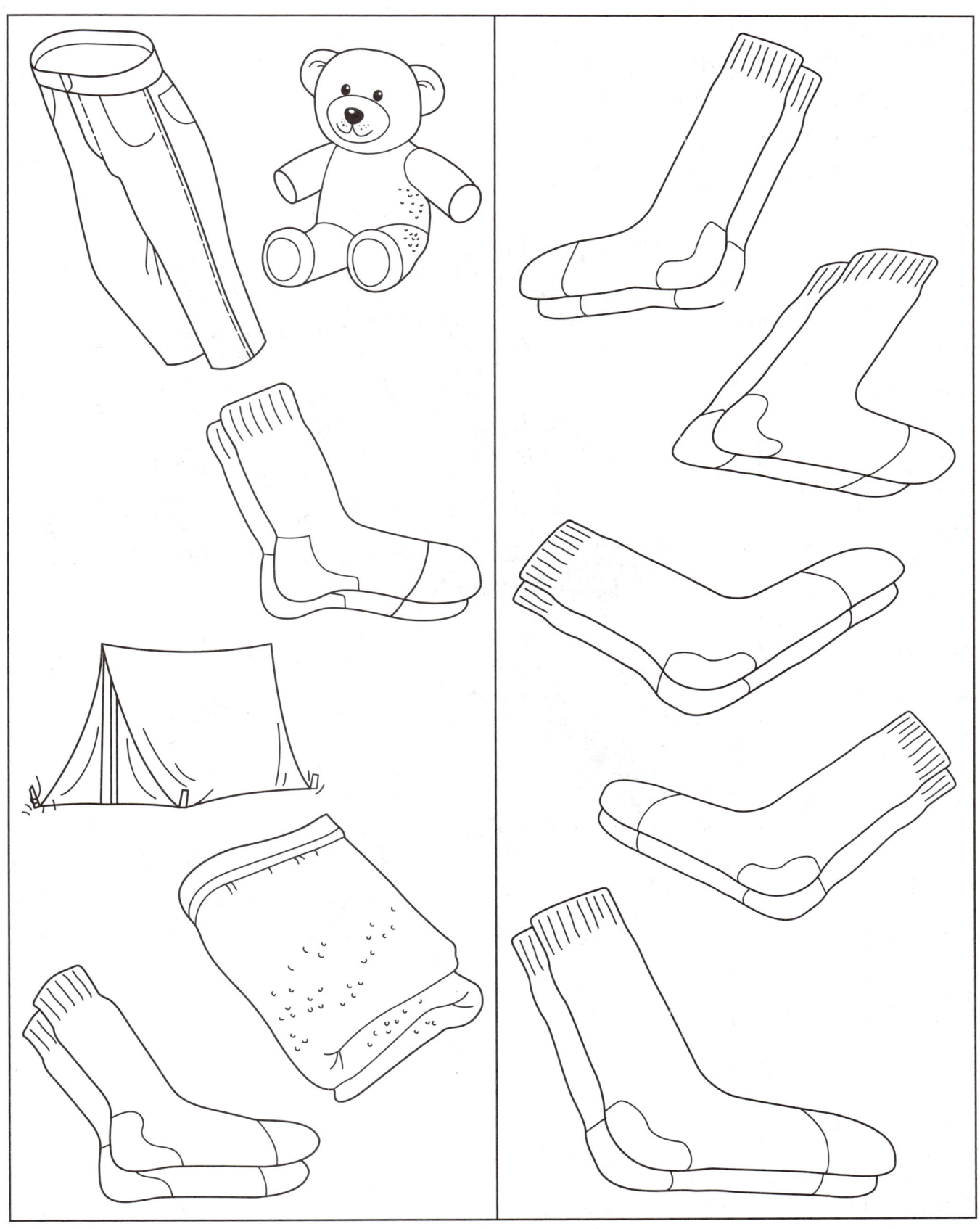

Side 1

books   reading   monkeys   bananas   eating

Side 2

Name _____

145

tools	materials	furniture
metal	screwdriver	_____
hammer	concrete	_____
chair	rake	_____
bed	desk	_____
cloth	wood	_____

Side 1

map

looking

driving

Side 2

Name _____

146

is to / are to   as   is to / are to

is to / are to   as   is to / are to

Side 1

field farmer chasing scared

Side 2

Name _____

147

plants	buildings	tools

tree — flower

fire station — house

ax — restaurant

pencil — scissors

grass — hammer

Side 1

Side 2

tiger rabbit flying reading
bird sleeping tree

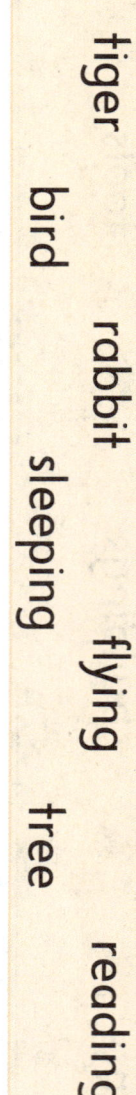

Name _____

148

Side 1

basketball   court   playing

Side 2

Name _____

143

Side 1

Name _____

True   False

1. A car has wheels. _____

2. A car has wings. _____

3. Cars are vehicles. _____

4. Cars can fly. _____

5. Cars can be clean. _____

| | big | | fat | | sick | | cry |
| small | | laugh | | yell | | thin | |

1. This shirt is too large.

S _____

O _____

2. She did not weep last night.

S _____

O _____

3. The skinny cat was sleeping.

S _____

O _____

Side 2

Name _____

| animals | furniture | containers |

cup _____   suitcase _____

couch _____   glass _____

goat _____   bed _____

giraffe _____   horse _____

table _____   box _____

Side 1

boys   playground   baseball

throwing   tall   playing

Side 2

PHOTO CREDITS

L085 Side 01 (1)Ingram Publishing/Alamy Images, (2)Ariel Skelley/Blend Images, (3)Photodisc/Getty Images, (4)©DreamPictures/Blend Images LLC, (5)Digital Vision/PunchStock, (6)science photo/Shutterstock, (7)Scanrail1/Shutterstock, (8)Jose Luis Pelaez Inc/Blend Images LLC, (9)steverts/iStock/Getty Images, (10)Bim/Getty Images, (11)Image Source, All rights reserved, (12)Monkey Business Images/Shutterstock; **L086 Side 01** (1)www.BillionPhotos.com/Shutterstock, (2)Visionsi/Shutterstock, (3)Ariel Skelley/Blend Images, (4)NASA, (5)©DreamPictures/Blend Images LLC, (6)Scanrail1/Shutterstock, (7)Imageshop/Alamy, (8)McGraw Hill, (9)CrackerClips/iStock/Getty Images, (10)Ingram Publishing/Alamy Images, (11)Konstantin Shaklein/3dsculptor/123RF; **L087 Side 01** (1)Lauren Burke/Photographer's Choice RF/Getty Images, (2)Mark Steinmetz/McGraw Hill, (3)Siede Preis/Getty Images, (4)Comstock Images/Alamy, (5)Mark Steinmetz/McGraw Hill, (6)nattanan726/Shutterstock, (7)clubfoto/E+/Getty Images, (8)lynx/iconotec.com/Glow Images, (9)McGraw Hill, (10)McGraw Hill, (11)Photographer's Choice/Getty Images, (12)Ingram Publishing/SuperStock, (13)Pixtal/AGE Fofostock, (14)deusexlupus/123RF; **L089 Side 01** (br)Gregor Schuster/Getty Images, (1)D. Hurst/Alamy, (2)surasaki/Shutterstock, (3)C Squared Studios/Photodisc/Getty Images, (4)Studiohio/McGraw Hill, (5)Ken Cavanagh/McGraw Hill, (6)Ingram Publishing/Fotosearch, (7)McGraw Hill, (8)Vladvm/Shutterstock, (9)photo one/Shutterstock, (10)Ken Cavanagh/McGraw Hill, (11)Perfect Picture Parts/Alamy Stock Photo, (12)McGraw Hill, (13)D. Hurst/Alamy, (14)Ingram Publishing/Age Fotostock, (15)Ingram Publishing/Fotosearch; **L092 Side 01** (tl)G.K. & Vikki Hart/Photodisc/Getty Images, (tcl)anat chant/Shutterstock, (tcr)G.K. & Vikki Hart/Photodisc/Getty Images, (tr)McGraw Hill, (tr)McGraw Hill, (cl)Judith Collins/Alamy Stock Photo, (cl)G.K. & Vikki Hart/Photodisc/Getty Images, (cl)G.K. & Vikki Hart/Getty Images, (cl)lynx/iconotec.com/Glow Images, (cl)Jules Frazier/Getty Images, (cl)Pixtal/AGE Fofostock, (c)Ingram Publishing/Alamy, (c)sevenke/Shutterstock, (c)Africa Studio/Shutterstock, (cr)ehtesham/Shutterstock, (cr)Ralf Hettler/E+/Getty Images, (bl)clubfoto/E+/Getty Images, (bcl)OJO Images Ltd/Alamy Stock Photo, (bcr)McGraw Hill, (br)belchonock ©123RF.com; **L094 Side 01** (tl)saiyood ©123RF.com, (tl)Cristian M. Vela/Alamy, (tcr)Joe DeGrandis/McGraw Hill, (tr)dra_schwartz/E+/Getty Images, (tr)Thomas Northcut/Photodisc/Getty Images, (cl)ansonsaw/E+/Getty Images, (cl)Vladimiroquai/iStock/Getty Images, (cr)aragami12345s/Shutterstock, (cr)Ingram Publishing/Alamy, (cr)Creative Crop/Digital Vision/Getty Images, (bl)Digital Vision/PunchStock, (bcl)ansonsaw/E+/Getty Images, (bcr)Artem Avetisyan/Shutterstock, (bcr)YAY Media AS/Alamy, (bcr)Cristian M. Vela/Alamy, (br)Brian Guest/Shutterstock, (bl)kali9/E+/Getty Images; **L095 Side 01** (tl)Ingram Publishing/age fotostock, (tcl)Ken Karp/McGraw Hill, (tcr)Quang Ho/Shutterstock, (tr)Ingram Publishing/Alamy Images, (cl)koosen/iStock/Getty Images, (cl)Siede Preis/Getty Images, (c)(c)Pixtal/SuperStock, (cr)maykal/123RF, (cr)DNY59/Getty Images, (cr)donatas1205 ©123RF.com, (cr)Quang Ho/Shutterstock, (cr)Ingram Publishing/Alamy Images, (c)Ken Karp/McGraw Hill, (cr)donatas1205 ©123RF.com, (bl)Spaces Images/Blend Images, (bl)maykal/123RF, (bl)Quang Ho/Shutterstock, (bcl)Saylakham/Shutterstock, (br)Kadir Barcin/E+/Getty Images; **L097 Side 03** (tl)Comstock Images/Alamy, (tcl)Ingram Publishing/Alamy Images, (tr)atoss/123, (cl)Praisaeng/Shutterstock, (cl)seregam/iStock/Getty Images, (c)McGraw Hill, (c)Boris Puhanic/Shutterstock, (c)Boris Puhanic/Shutterstock, (cr)C Squared Studios/Getty Images, (cr)Lev Kropotov/Getty Images, (cr)Ingram Publishing/Age Fotostock, (cr)Alex Cao/Photodisc/Getty Images, (cr)Lauren Burke/Photographer's Choice RF/Getty Images, (cr)PhotoAlto/SuperStock, (cr)Ken Karp/McGraw Hill, (bl)lynx/iconotec.com/Glow Images, (bl)atoss/123, (bcl)Author's Image/Glow Images, (bcr)Hanis/E+/Getty Images, (br)Jupiterimages/Photos.com/360/Getty Images; **L098 Side 02** (tl)Pixtal/age fotostock, (tcr)Pixtal/AGE Fotostock, (tr)Photodisc/Getty Images, (cl)Pixtal/AGE Fotostock, (cl)NIPAPORN PANYACHAROEN/Shutterstock, (cl)Siede Preis/Getty Images, (cl)Lauren Burke/Photographer's Choice RF/Getty Images, (cl)Judith Collins/Alamy Stock Photo, (c)Mark Steinmetz, (cr)Ilene Macdonald/Alamy, (cr)Steve Heap/Shutterstock, (cr)McGraw Hill, (bl)G.K. & Vikki Hart/Getty Images, (bl)lynx/iconotec.com/Glow Images, (bcl)Imageshop/Alamy, (bcr)McGraw Hill, (br)McGraw Hill; **L100 Side 01** (tl)C Squared Studios/Photodisc/Getty Images, (tcl)popovaphoto/iStock/Getty Images Plus, (tcr)Steve Heap/Shutterstock, (tr)FatCamera/Getty Images, (cl)McGraw Hill/JW Ramsey, (cl)McGraw Hill, (cl)Ken Cavanagh/McGraw Hill, (cl)Irina Rogova/Shutterstock, (c)C Squared Studios/Photodisc/Getty Images, (cr)Lecneo/iStock/Getty Images, (cr)Indian collections/Shutterstock, (bl)Ingram Publishing/Age Fotostock, (bl)G.K. Vikki Hart/Getty Images, (bl)Ken Cavanagh/McGraw Hill, (bcl)Rob Marmion/Shutterstock, (bcr)Mark Steinmetz, (br)Ken Cavanagh/McGraw Hill, (br)Ken Cavanagh/McGraw Hill; **L102 Side 02** (tl)fergregory/123RF.com, (tcr)Jenoche/123RF, (tr)Beathan/SuperStock, (cl)©Steve Hamblin/Alamy Stock Photo, (cl)Getty Images/fStop, (cl)Image Source, All rights reserved, (c)Tsekhmister/Shutterstock, (cr)Steven Schleuning, (cr)Brian Guest/Shutterstock, (bl)GlobalP/Getty Images, (bl)StompingGirl/Shutterstock, (bl)Photodisc/Getty Images, (bcl)Paul Burns/Blend Images LLC, (bcr)stefan77/123RF, (bcr)rawpixel/123RF, (bcr)NASA, (br)Le Do/123RF; **L103 Side 03** (1)©Jose Luis Pelaez Inc/Blend Images LLC, (2)Bullstar/Shutterstock, (3)HONGQI ZHANG/123RF, (4)LifetimeStock/Shutterstock, (5)fortovik/Shutterstock, (6)rawpixel/123RF, (7)Comstock Images/Alamy Images, (8)Shutterstock, (9)Peter Steiner/Alamy, (10)scottff72 ©123RF.com, (11)Image Source, All rights reserved, (12)©Randy Lincks/CORBIS, (13)NNehring/E+/Getty Images, (14)Denys Kurylow/123RF, (15)Peterspiro iStock/Getty Images; **L105 Side 01** (1)JGI/Tom Grill/Getty Images, (2)Eric Isselee/Shutterstock, (3)T.A. Clarey/Shutterstock, (4)zhao jiankang/123RF, (5)Shutterstock, (6)wavebreakmedia/Shutterstock, (7)fifoprod ©123RF.com, (8)Ingram Publishing/SuperStock, (9)Victoria Blackie/Photodisc/Getty Images, (10)tanakrit tipkanok/123RF, (11)Image Source, (12)zhao jiankang/123RF, (13)Design Pics/Corey Hochachka; **L107 Side 02** (tl)AS Food studio/Shutterstock, (tcl)Digital Zoo/Photodisc/Getty Images, (tcr)Comstock/Stockbyte/Getty Images, (tr)Michiel de Wit/Shutterstock, (tr)mashe/Shutterstock, (c)Holly Curry/McGraw Hill, (c)Alex Cao/Photodisc/Getty Images, (c)I. Rosenbaum/PhotoAlto, (cr)BanksPhotos/E+/Getty Images, (cr)Andrew Ilyasov/E+/Getty Images, (cr)Juniors Bildarchiv/Alamy Stock Photo, (cr)nattanan726/Shutterstock, (cr)ronniechua/123RF, (bl)Ingram Publishing/age fotostock, (bl)Ingram Publishing/SuperStock, (bcl)Suntipab/iStock/Getty Images, (bcr)lynx/iconotec.com/Glow Images, (bcr)lynx/iconotec.com/Glow Images, (bcr)Jacques Cornell/McGraw Hill, (bcr)Ingram Publishing/Age Fotostock, (br)G.K. & Vikki Hart/Getty Images; **L108 Side 01** (tl)Eric Isselee/Shutterstock, (tcr)Siede Preis/Getty Images, (tr)Judith Collins/Alamy Stock Photo, (cl)PhotoDisc/Getty Images, Inc., (cl)Lars Christensen/Shutterstock, (cl)arlindo71/E+/Getty Images, (c)fifoprod ©123RF.com, (c)Evgeny Karandaev/Shutterstock, (c)yevgeniy11/Shutterstock, (cr)photomaster/Shutterstock, (cr)withGod/Shutterstock, (bcl)Steve Hamblin/Alamy Stock Photo, (bcr)McGraw Hill, (br)Eureka/Alamy, (br)G.K. & Vikki Hart/Getty Images, (br)Photodisc/Getty Images, (br)Photodisc/Getty Images; **L110 Side 01** (tl)Comstock Images/Alamy, (tr)Hanis/E+/Getty Images, (cl)McGraw Hill, (cl)koosen/iStock/Getty Images, (c)Ingram Publishing/Alamy Images, (cr)Mark Steinmetz/McGraw Hill Companies, (cr)Lev Kropotov/Alamy, (bl)Rob Marmion/Shutterstock, (bcl)Maltaguy1/iStock/Getty Images, (br)lynx/iconotec.com/Glow Images, (br)Artem Avetisyan/Shutterstock, (br)Thomas Northcut/Photodisc/Getty Images, (br)C Squared Studios/Photodisc/Getty Images; **L112 Side 02** (1)McGraw Hill, (2)McGraw Hill, (3)Don Farrall/Getty Images, (4)Don Farrall/Getty Images, (5)Siede Preis/Getty Images, (6)G.K. & Vikki Hart/Photodisc/Getty Images, (7)G.K. & Vikki Hart/Photodisc/Getty Images, (8)Butterfly Hunter/Shutterstock, (9)cynoclub/Shutterstock, (10)Ingram Publishing, (11)Evgeny Karandaev/Shutterstock, (12)Christopher Kerrigan/McGraw Hill, (13)Lauren Burke/Photographer's Choice RF/Getty Images, (14)Alex Cao/Photodisc/Getty Images, (15)Tsekhmister/Shutterstock; **L114 Side 01** (1)holbox/Shutterstock, (2)Paul Burns/Blend Images LLC, (3)Radius Images/Alamy, (4)Peter Steiner/Alamy, (5)Kostic Dusan/123RF, (6)PBNJ Productions/Blend Images LLC, (7)G.K. & Vikki Hart/Photodisc/Getty Images, (8)Evgenii Skidanov/123RF, (9)MaxyM/Shutterstock, (10)peterspiro/iStock/360/Getty Images, (11)Comstock/Getty Images; **L115 Side 02** (1)popovaphoto ©123RF.com, (2)McGraw Hill, (3)Siede Preis/Getty Images, (4)Ken Cavanagh/McGraw Hill, (5)Ken Cavanagh/McGraw Hill, (6)Ingram Publishing/Age Fotostock, (7)purplequeue/Shutterstock, (8)Comstock Images/Getty Images, (9)Ken Cavanagh/McGraw Hill, (10)Richard Hutchings, (11)Konstantin Gushcha/Shutterstock; **L117 Side 01** (1)lunamarina/Shutterstock, (2)Ingram Publishing/Age Fotostock, (3)lunamarina/Shutterstock, (4)Ingram Publishing/Age Fotostock, (5)Marcin Perkowski/Shutterstock, (6)Oksana Tkachuk/123RF, (7)G.K. & Vikki Hart/Photodisc/Getty Images, (8)McGraw Hill, (9)Siede Preis/Photodisc/PunchStock, (10)mashe/Shutterstock, (11)Pixtal/AGE Fotostock; **L119 Side 01** (1)Purestock/SuperStock, (2)Keith Homan/123RF, (3)Purestock/SuperStock, (4)Keith Homan/123RF, (5)George Doyle & Ciaran Griffin, (6)rawpixel/123RF, (7)James R. Martin/Shutterstock, (8)Pixtal/AGE Fotostock, (9)thesupe87 ©123RF.com, (10)ColorBlind Images/Blend Images LLC, (11)Vevchic/Shutterstock; **L123 Side 01** (1)lynx/iconotec.com/Glow Images, (2)Praisaeng/Shutterstock, (3)McGraw Hill, (4)Eye-Stock/Alamy Stock Photo, (5)C Squared Studios/Getty Images, (6)Lev Kropotov/Shutterstock, (7)Ken Karp/McGraw Hill, (8)Comstock/Stockbyte/Getty Images, (9)McGraw Hill, (10)McGraw Hill, (11)Ingram Publishing/Alamy Images; **L128 Side 01** (1)Thawat Tanhai/123RF, (2)Amanda Rohde/iStock/Getty Images, (3)Ken Cavanagh/McGraw Hill, (4)Lan Images/Shutterstock, (5)D. Hurst/Alamy Stock Photo, (6)Lauren Burke/Photographer's Choice RF/Getty Images, (7)malerapaso/E+/Getty Images, (8)Stockphoto/Getty Images, (9)Andrey_Kuzmin/iStock/Getty Images, (10)Tom Wang/Alamy, (11)Michael J. Shirey; **L143 Side 01** (1)Topconcept/Shutterstock, (2)Jirsak/iStock/Getty Images, (3)Ingram Publishing/SuperStock, (4)Nerthuz/iStock/Getty Images, (5)Comstock/SuperStock, (6)Photodisc/Getty Images, (7)MaxyM/Shutterstock, (8)Sava Alexandru/Getty Images, (9)William Perugini/Shutterstock, (10)Somchai_Stock/Shutterstock, (11)TFoxFoto/Shutterstock, (12)PBNJ Productions/Blend Images; **L146 Side 01** (tcl)Steve Heap/Shutterstock, (tcr)ansonsaw/E+/Getty Images, (t)sakhorn/Shutterstock, (cl)Allan Swart/Alamy Stock Photo, (c)Ratthaphong Ekariyasap/Shutterstock, (c)Ingram Publishing/Alamy Stock Photo, (c)William Ryall, (c)Wealthylady/Shutterstock, (cr)Creative Crop/Digital Vision/Getty Images, (cr)Mike Kiev/iStock/Getty Images, (cr)C Squared Studios/Getty Images, (tl)Lecneo/iStock/Getty Images, (bcr)Image Source, All rights reserved, (bcr)G.K. & Vikki Hart/Getty Images, (bcr)Ilene MacDonald/Alamy, (bcr)Steve Heap/Shutterstock, (br)saiyood ©123RF.com, (br)Vladimiroquai/iStock/Getty Images, (br)ansonsaw/E+/Getty Images, (tl)Ryan McVay/Getty Images.